Making and Playing
MUSICAL INSTRUMENTS

DAVID TENIERS d.J. pinxt.

Jack Botermans, Herman Dewit, Hans Goddefroy

Making and Playing
MUSICAL INSTRUMENTS

Text: Afke den Boer and Margot de Zeeuw
Translation: Anthony Burrett
Working drawings: Piet Hohmann

University of Washington Press
Seattle

Editing and composition: Jack Botermans
Consultants: Herman Dewit and Hans
Goddefroy
Text: Afke den Boer† and Margot de Zeeuw
Translation: Anthony Burrett
Text editor: Jan Guus Waldorp
Working drawings: Piet Hohmann
Models of musical instruments
   Built or loaned by Herman Dewit and Hans
Goddefroy
   Photographed by Jack Botermans
Cover illustration: Dominique Ampe
Printing: Druckhaus Meyer GmbH, Germany
Typesetting: Grafisch bedrijf Essay,
Valkenswaard
Lithography: Fotolitho Boan bv, Utrecht

Contents

There are thousands of musical instruments throughout the world.
This book contains a selection of them. The instruments are divided
into the following categories: aerophones. idiophones,
membranophones and chordophones. The selection of instruments in
each category is presented in an increasing degree of difficulty in both
making and playing.

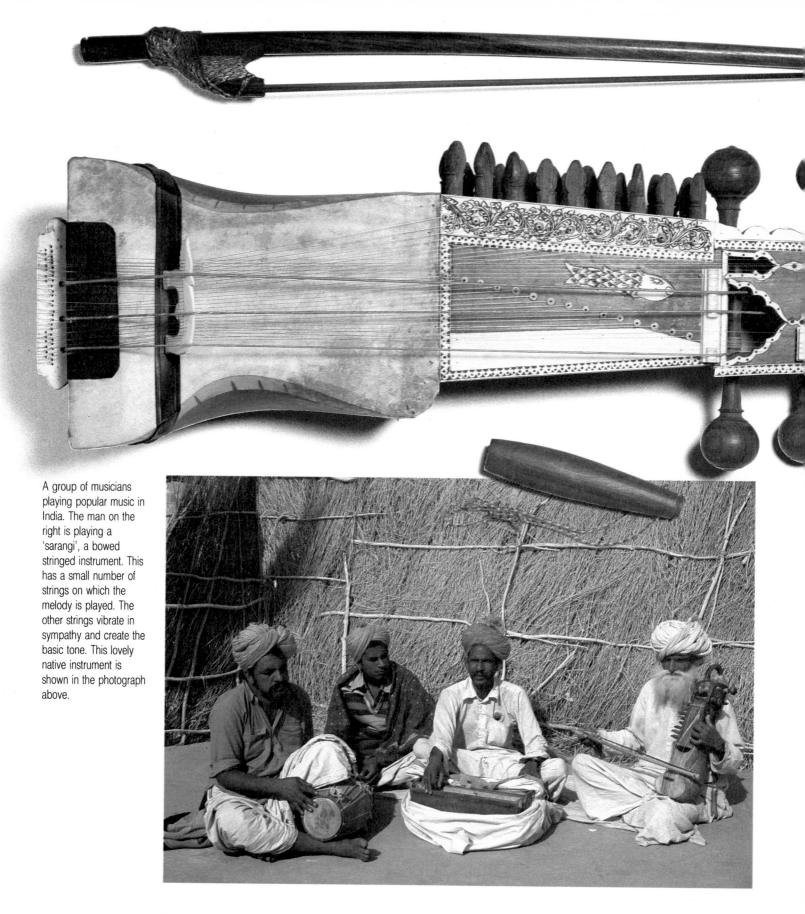

A group of musicians playing popular music in India. The man on the right is playing a 'sarangi', a bowed stringed instrument. This has a small number of strings on which the melody is played. The other strings vibrate in sympathy and create the basic tone. This lovely native instrument is shown in the photograph above.

6

Introduction

This book − Making and Playing Musical Instruments − offers you a unique opportunity to express your creativity. The book is so constructed that you can begin by making or playing either a simple instrument or a more difficult one, depending on your knowledge of music and your skill in do-it-yourself techniques. The most difficult instrument to make is the hurdy gurdy. This offers a real challenge but the result, both aesthetically and musically, will far exceed your expectations.

People have made music from the very earliest times. Sometimes this music had a religious meaning. In the Middle Ages, music often served as a vehicle to remember and pass on traditional stories. Over the centuries, thousands of different instruments have been made in every corner of the world. Some of these have been lost; others, often in adapted form, are still used today.

In this book we would also like to introduce you to the world of folk instruments. You do not need to be an expert or scholar to make and play such an instrument. On the other hand, making and playing them will teach you a great deal about this subject.

This book contains some forty instruments, divided into the categories: aerophones, idiophones, membranophones and chordophones. How the instruments are built and played is clearly explained in text and illustration. Nonetheless, you will notice that these instructions are sufficiently flexible for you to make use of your own creative abilities. This means that you can make your own personal version − in shape, design and decoration − of any particular instrument. Making and playing instruments − like drawing and painting − is a highly personal matter.

In principle, you only need a small number of basic tools to make the instruments described. A few are illustrated on pages 8 and 9.
A description of the materials required can be found on pages 10 and 11.

Playing the instrument
You must not expect to be able to play all the instruments you make immediately. To do this, practise is necessary. The principles and techniques of playing (fingering, for example) described in this book, however, will set you on your way. We know from our own experience how fantastic it is to actually be able to play an instrument which you have built yourself.
We wish you every success!

Tools

When making this book, we began with the assumption that you possess a few basic woodworking tools. On these pages you can see a number of tools which are useful for specific tasks.

On this page are shown those tools which are most necessary to build the instruments described in this book.

1. Conical gouge
Used to make conical holes for tuning pins.

2. Sharpener
Is the same size as the gouge and is used for making the tuning pins themselves.

3 and 4. Notching and cutting knives
Used for decorative incised work and cutting windows. You can make these knives yourself by grinding down diagonally both sides of an ordinary knife. (see illustration).

5. Compass(es)
Used for determining the circumference and position of finger holes, frets and holes for tuning pins.

6. Small tenon saw
Used, among other things, for cutting joints and for making grooves in bridges and fretboards.

7. Whittling knife
Used for removing burrs inside finger holes of the various flute instruments.

8. Marking gauge
Used to mark distances and positions on wood. The scratches it makes can easily be removed later with sandpaper.

9. 'Witch's tooth'
Is a special plane used for smoothing larger areas. It is used as a basic plane but also works as a scraper.

10. Engagement clamp
This is the ideal type of clamp to use when making musical instruments because it

does not allow the parts you are working with to slip or twist.

11. Spring clamps
These clamps are suitable for holding small joints in place when glueing.

12. Try square
Used for marking right angles and lines.

13. Steel rule
Useful in the making of any instrument. All the measurements in this book are given in millimetres.

14. Pencil
An essential tool in the making of any instrument! It is best to use a pencil with an HB degree of hardness.

15. Deep engagement clamp
A simple clamp used for holding basic right-angled wood joints when glueing.

16. Gouges
For cutting grooves and hollows in wood.

17. (Brad)awl
Used to prick starting points in places where holes must be drilled.

18. Abrasive blocks
Blocks in every shape and form are used to sandpaper specific surfaces. They can easily be made by glueing sandpaper of various grades on slats of wood.

19. Wood planes
These can be bought in all sizes. Essential in the building of wooden musical instruments.

20. Scrapers
Used to scrape hollows in flat pieces of wood.

21. Sanding block
Can easily be made by wrapping a piece of sandpaper around a block of cork or wood. Used to smooth large areas.

Materials

On these pages are some of the materials which are often used in the building of musical instruments. These materials are not only used to make the instrument described in this book, but also by professional instrument makers.

Of course, for any particular instrument (the talharpa or long-necked lute, for example), you are quite free to choose a better (often more expensive) type of wood than the one suggested.

On these pages are illustrated the types of wood which are the most used in building musical instruments. Other materials, such as bone, ivory or horn, are also illustrated.

1. Ivory
Used to make tuning pins, bridges, ferrules for flutes and bagpipes, small turned work, transverse flute.

2. Cow's horn
Used for flutes, pegs, ferrules for bagpipes and transverse flutes, small turned work.

3. Bone
Clappers, inlaid work, bridges (for the hummel-a Swedish board zither) ferrules for wind instruments, various pegs.

4. Cedar
Origin: the west of North America.
Color: varies; light yellowish-brown, reddish-brown, salmon and chocolate-brown.
Properties: fine, straight grain, fairly soft (s.g. 0.60), not particularly strong, good durability.
Uses: ideal for the body of recorders.

5. Maple
(note: sycamore is a very similar wood)
Origin: Canada, many European countries.
Color: Whitish-yellow with a silky gloss. German maple is less glossy.
Properties: very fine, closed grain, moderately hard, not very heavy (s.g. 0.60), warps hardly at all, quite flexible.
Uses: ideal for soundboxes of stringed instruments (for example, guitar, violin, hummel, hurdy gurdy).

6. Rosewood *(Santos)*
12. Rosewood *(Honduras)*
Origin: Brazil, Honduras, Madagascar, India, Java, Sri Lanka.
Color: substantial differences in color, depending on the origin. Brownish-red to purplish-brown, sometimes with black veins.
Properties: fine grain, solid, strong and heavy (s.g. 1.00); warps hardly at all.
Uses: chiefly used for recorders, flutes, soundboxes for guitars, xylophone staves, tuning pins.

7. Pine
Origin: North, Central, East and South-east Europe.
Color: whitish-yellow with a high silvery gloss.
Properties: fine growth rings, strong, tough, not heavy (s.g. 0.50).
Uses: an ideal wood for the upper panels of the violin, guitar and hummel; keyboard instruments and xylophone staves.

1

2 3 4 5 6 7 8

8. Pear

Origin: West-Europe.
Color: reddish-brown.
Properties: very fine closed grain, solid, strong and tough, fairly heavy (s.g. 0.75), dried and seasoned pear wood does not warp.
Uses: flutes, hummels, all turned work.

9. Walnut

Origin: Europe, America and the Middle East.
Color: The color can vary according to the country of origin. Dutch walnut is lightish-grey in color, occasionally beautifully dark-brown colored or veined walnut can be found. French and German walnut is more greyish-brown in color, often with darker brown or chocolate-brown veins. American walnut is more purplish-brown to chocolate-brown in color.
Turkish and Persian walnut (often known as Italian walnut because it is imported through Italy), is a lovely dark brown.
Uses: soundboxes for folk instruments such as the hurdy gurdy, hummel and drums, various turned work.

10. Ebony

Origin: Zaire, South-east Asia, Sri Lanka and Madagascar.
Color: black to bluish-black. Indonesian ebony is sometimes rather brownish in color.
Properties: extremely closed grain, hard, very heavy (s.g. 1.2), extremely durable, does not work or warp. Sold by weight.
Uses: fingerboards for stringed instruments, flutes, clarinet, inlaid work, oboe, small turned work, pegs, tuning pins, keys for keyboard instruments.

11. Box wood

Origin: countries around the Mediterranean Sea, England, the Pyrenees, Turkey.
Color: golden-yellow and smooth, sometimes with small knots and burrs. Darkens with age.
Properties: very fine, closed grain. Hard, fairly heavy (s.g. 0.85-1.0). Takes years to dry thoroughly. After drying it works hardly at all. If box wood dries too quickly, it will split. Sometimes mistakenly known as palm wood.
Uses: flutes and various other wind instruments, tuning pins, small turned work, hurdy gurdy pegs, soles of smoothing planes, bagpipes, inlaid work.

12. Rosewood *(Honduras)* see 6.

13. Plum

Origin: many European countries.
Color: reddish-brown, perhaps with purplish veins, lightly stained.
Properties: fine closed grain, relatively hard and tough, not heavy (s.g. 0.55-0.75).
Uses: flutes, soundboxes for the hummel, hurdy gurdy, guitar; tuning pins, turned work.

14. Yew

Origin: Central and South Europe.
Color: whitish-yellow.
Properties: Rougher in texture than pine, fine long fibres, strong, springy, not heavy (s.g. 0.45).
Yew wood does not contain resin. Knots and burrs are round and harder than those in pine wood and are often loose.
Tougher than pine.
Uses: small flutes, lute frames, inlaid work, small turned work.

15. An example of quarter-sawn timber.

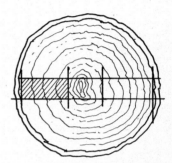

The illustration shows from which section of the trunk quarter-sawn timber is derived.

15

9   10   11   12   13   14

Aerophones

Aerophones are musical instruments in which sounds are produced by the vibration of air. Because air can be made to vibrate in a number of different ways, aerophones form a large and versatile family. Flutes, recorders, panpipes and ocarinas are among the best-known aerophones, but clarinets, trumpets, horns, bagpipes, accordions and organs also belong to this group of instruments.

Blowing a flute is closely related to singing. A flute is a sort of extension to the breath and the voice. One-pitch flutes (simple whistles), made from bones, have been known since pre-historic times. Since then every culture has accorded the flute with magical powers. The sound of the flute could conciliate the gods, calm demons, summon love, conjure up storms, make the fields fruitful and accompany the dead on their journey to the next world. Of course, even in those days, the flute was an excellent means of exchanging signals over great distances.

While drums in Africa and gongs and lutes in Asia form an important part of the cultures, in Europe wind instruments have always played a conspicuous role. The number of different wind instruments existing in our Western culture — many derived from instruments of other cultures — is remarkable. The bagpipes are one of the best-known folk instruments in Europe and although the mouth organ and accordion were invented relatively recently they have since played an important role in Western folk music.

Four examples of endblown flutes. The top one is made of a synthetic material, the second and third are metal. The bottom one, played with one hand, is made of bamboo.

How aerophones work

All the musical instruments in the aerophone family work according to the same principle. The pitch and the tone quality are a result of the way in which the air vibrates, the shape and length of the instrument and the material from which it is made.

Making the air vibrate

The various types of aerophone are classified according to the manner in which the air is made to vibrate.

Vibrations can be created by blowing air against a sharp edge (A and B), as occurs in many types of flutes. A sound can be produced in this way from keys and bottles.

Vibrations can also be produced by blowing against a tongue or reed cut from a cylindrical tube. This is how sound is produced in, for example, the clarinet and bagpipes. There are various combinations, such as the single reed (C), the double reed (D) or the free reed (E). In cup mouthpiece instruments, the player creates the vibrations with the lips (F).

In a free-standing aerophone (G), the air vibrates around the instrument itself.

Body shapes

Most aerophones are tubular in shape. The tube can be cylindrical (A) (as in the elder flute and reed pipe), tapering (B) (as in the recorder) or flared (C) (as in the oboe). The vessel body (D) – the ocarina, for example – is found less frequently.

Ocarinas and cow's horn flutes are members of the closed chamber family of aerophones.

Pitch

The length of the tube in which the air is vibrating determines the length of the sound waves and, therefore, the pitch.

Any tube produces a pitch appropriate to its length and this is known as the basic pitch or fundamental. A 500 mm tube (A) produces a fundamental which is an octave higher than that produced by a 1000 mm tube. An open (unstopped) 500 mm tube will sound an octave higher than a closed (stopped) 500 mm tube. The internal diameter of the tube also has an influence on the basic pitch. The greater the internal diameter, the shorter the tube must be in order to produce the same basic pitch.

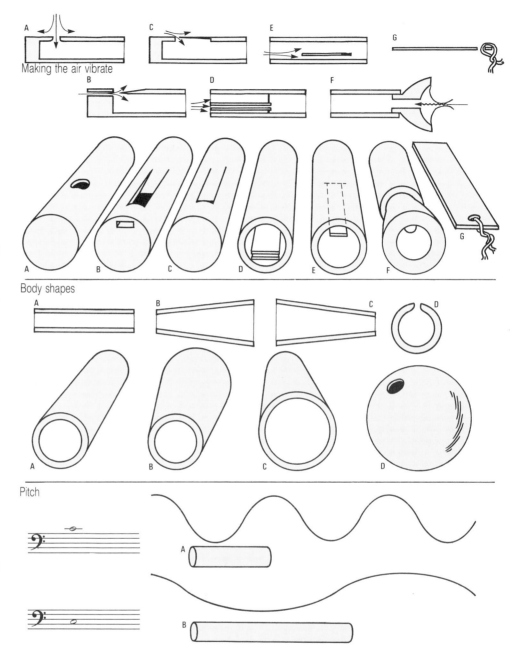

Making the air vibrate

Body shapes

Pitch

The basic pitch can be tuned by shortening the tube little by little. When tuning, you must take into account the fact that the basic pitch of a tube without finger holes is different from that of the same tube with holes. This is because the holes slightly increase the internal volume. A basic pitch of C, for example, can almost become a basic pitch of B when finger holes are added.

Shortening an instrument – a flute for example – raises the pitch. Do this a tiny bit at a time, so that the pitch changes only a fraction. If the pitch is too high, it can be lowered by sticking a little ball of wax in the mouth of the instrument.

The harmonic series

Aerophones

The harmonic series

When air is made to vibrate, it vibrates not only as a whole – the fundamental – but also in sections – secondary vibrations.

These additional pitches are known as harmonics and are produced by increasing the intensity of the air stream so that the air vibrates more quickly in the tube.

These harmonics occur in a particular sequence, known as the harmonic series. The distance between two tones of a harmonic series is fixed, but the actual pitch is determined by the size and shape of the tube.

Altering the pitch

The principle of producing pitches other than the fundamental and the harmonic series consists of shortening or lengthening the stream of air in the tube. The stream of air is shortened when the air can escape through holes situated at the lower the end of the tube (A) – as in the flute.

Different pitches are produced by allowing the air to escape through different holes.

The stream of air can be lengthened by the use of a simple slide mechanism. A narrower tube is inserted inside a wider one, so that when necessary it is possible to lengthen the tube (B) – as in the trombone.

Another way to lengthen the stream of air is by using crooks or valves to divert the air through an extra length of tubing (C) – as in the trumpet.

Tone color

Every aerophone has its own distinctive sound quality or 'tone color'. Not only has every material – and every type of wood – its own tone color, but the sound is also influenced by the length, shape and thickness of the tube and the way in which the air is made to vibrate. The sound of a reed pipe, for example, is totally different to that of a flute made from elder wood.

Any pitch which is played is colored by the harmonics associated with that pitch.

These harmonics are determined by the shape of the tube. The conical tube of the oboe, for example, emphasizes the lower harmonics (A). The stopped cylindrical tube of the clarinet, in contrast, emphasizes the odd-numbered harmonics (B).

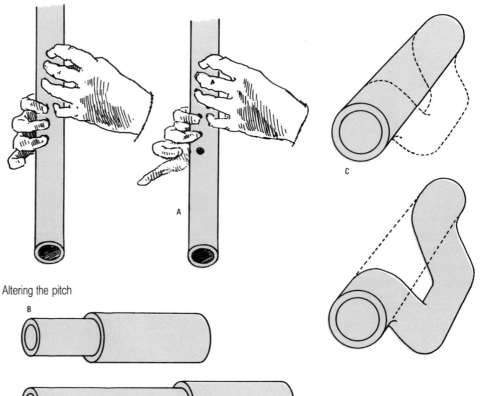

Altering the pitch

Tone color

The elder flute

The elder flute is a simple recorder. According to one old European definition, someone who plays this instrument is a n'er-do-well, a rake who light-heartedly wanders through life playing a merry tune. This flute belongs to the family of fipple flutes and has been made and played for centuries. The upper end of the tube is plugged with a block of wood or cork — the fipple — and a slit between this and the mouthpiece forms the windway. Air is made to vibrate by directing it along the windway against the sharp lip of a hole known as the 'window'.

For an internal diameter K, apply the following dimensions:

K	14	13.5	12	12	11.5	10.5
A	22	22	22	22	22	22
B	5.5	5	5	5	4.5	4.5
C	161	141.5	123.5	115	100	94
D	187	163	144	135	118.5	110
E	213	187.5	167	155	137	126
F	241	211.5	189.5	175	155	141.5
G	262	233	207	193	170.5	155
H	295	262	232	215	192.5	174
J	345	307	270	255	226	204
L	9	8	8	7.5	6.5	6.5

Preparing the wood
A thin branch of the elder tree or bush — which grows in most countries — is used to make this flute. The best season to cut the wood is winter because then it dries out more quickly.
The length and the internal diameter of the pipe are important in determining the pitch of an elder flute. A long, wide pipe gives a low pitch; a short, narrow one gives a high pitch. You must therefore choose your branch carefully. The most suitable is one of approximately 15 to 18 mm in thickness with walls of about 4 mm and 10 mm of pith.

Immediately after the branch has been cut, the pith must be removed with a long, sharp-pointed tool, such as a knitting needle. Within a few hours the pith attaches itself to the inner wall and then becomes very difficult to extract. If the branch is left in the freezer for a few days, however, the pith again becomes easy to remove. The bark can be left in place. After the pith has been removed, leave the branch to dry out for a few weeks. This ensures that the finished instrument will not warp or split and become out of tune.

The quickest method of drying the wood is to leave it outside for a week, followed by a week inside and a further week on the central heating. If you try to dry the wood directly on a radiator, it will split.

The window and the lip
The real work begins when the wood is well dried out. Every branch is thicker towards the base and is therefore somewhat conical in shape. The mouthpiece will be at the thicker end, the mouth at the thinner end. First, the inner wall must be cleaned and smoothed. You can do this with a small wire brush or a cloth wrapped round a stick. The smoother the inner wall, the purer the tone will be.
The best-figured side of the wood will be the upper side of the flute. Use a pencil to mark the position of the window. This is approx. 22 mm from the end (see table).
The shape of the window and the sharpness of the lip have great influence on the tone color. A sharp lip gives the flute a sharp sound with many overtones. A blunt lip, on the other hand, gives a flatter sound. A narrow window also creates overtones and gives a fairly thin sound. A wide window gives fundamental tones. Novice instrument makers are therefore advised to cut a fairly small, shallow window.

When the center point and dimensions of the window have been determined, it can be cut out with a hobby knife. The length is about twice the thickness of the pipe wall.
Do not cut too deeply. If the window is too small it can always be enlarged by further cutting or filing. This is much easier than making it smaller! The walls of the window are filed and sandpapered smooth.

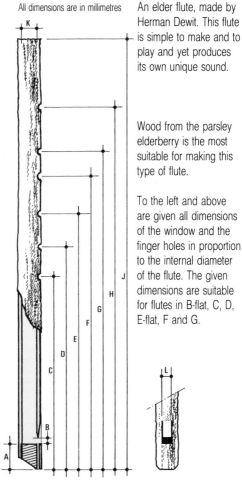

All dimensions are in millimetres

An elder flute, made by Herman Dewit. This flute is simple to make and to play and yet produces its own unique sound.

Wood from the parsley elderberry is the most suitable for making this type of flute.

To the left and above are given all dimensions of the window and the finger holes in proportion to the internal diameter of the flute. The given dimensions are suitable for flutes in B-flat, C, D, E-flat, F and G.

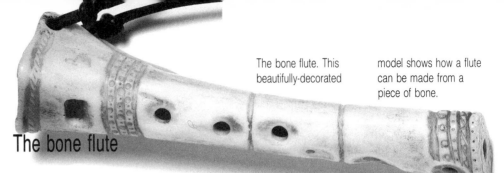

The bone flute. This beautifully-decorated model shows how a flute can be made from a piece of bone.

The windway

Using a drill which is approximately 1 mm thicker than the internal diameter, bore a clean, round hole in the end of the pipe up to the beginning of the window. File out a shallow channel – the windway – inside the pipe from the end up to the window. This should be the same width as the window (see table and illustration (L). A wooden stop or cork, also with a windway filed in the upper surface, is now fitted into the end of the tube. Adjust the stop until the windway is level with the sharp lip of the window and then glue it in position. The end is now cut and filed to form the mouth piece of your flute (see illustration).

The finger holes

Using a red-hot awl, burn the six finger holes, one by one (see Tuning below), into the upper surface of the flute. (If a drill is used for this operation, it forms burrs on the inner surface – and these are almost impossible to remove cleanly). The larger the hole, the higher the pitch. Therefore it is sensible to begin with a small hole and then enlarge it carefully.

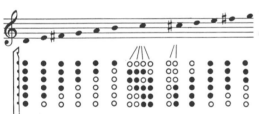

Tuning
The flute is first tuned to the basic pitch, either by ear or with a tuning fork. The first finger hole is then made. If this lowers the pitch, then the body of the flute is shortened until the pitch is again true. Then the second finger hole is made and the pitch and both the finger holes checked. If necessary these are also adjusted. This process is repeated for the other finger holes.

Fingering
The fingering of this flute is the same as that for the Pied Piper's flute or fife (see table). Holes in black are covered with a finger. Of course, it takes practise to be able to play the given scale.

Playing
The blowing technique for playing this flute is similar to that for the recorder. Practice the scale using the fingering system which is illustrated above.

The bone flute

Bones have an unpleasant smell and are rather messy to prepare. Making a bone flute therefore requires perseverance. But once you have made one, it will last you for millions of years!

Preparing the bone

The thigh bone of the back leg of a sheep is used for this flute. These can be readily obtained at an abattoire or from your local butcher. From the illustration it can be seen clearly that the window is positioned at the broader end of the bone.

This is sawn off to expose the marrow. Saw narrow strips of bone from the other end until a small hole – approx. 6 mm in diameter – becomes visible.

The bone should now be cleaned thoroughly in hot water – not boiling water, as this tenderizes the bone. The marrow can easily be removed with a small, stiff brush. Soak the bone in a bleach solution for a few hours and it will become beautifully white.

The window and windway

The window is first bored in the bone using a small-sized drill and then filed out (see the illustration and instructions for the elder flute).

Push clay into the bone to the level of the front of the window and smear butter inside the mouthpiece. Now pour gypsum (plaster of Paris) into the mouthpiece. Push a knotted cord into the wet plaster. Due to the butter smeared inside the mouthpiece, the hardened plaster plug can easily be removed by pulling gently on this cord. Use a stick to push the clay out of the bone.

The windway is now carefully filed in both the plaster plug and the inside of the bone (see illustration) and any remaining butter wiped out of the mouthpiece. The plug (the fipple) is now fixed in position with good-quality wood glue.

Finger holes

Hold the flute to your lips and mark the positions of the six finger holes and the thumb hole. Because the bone is so small these holes may not be in a straight line.

Ensure that the first hole is not too close to the window. Make the holes with a small drill and enlarge them with a file until the required pitch is obtained. Holes which are too big can be stopped with beeswax.

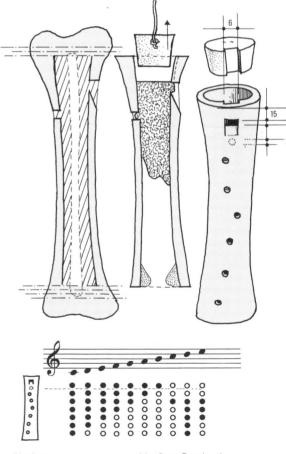

Playing
The bone flute is played in the same way as the elder flute. Practice the scale using the table illustrated above.

The cow's horn flute

In the early phase, making a cow's horn flute demands even more perseverance than making a bone flute! The end result, however, is an unusual instrument which gives excellent results.
Some animal horns are beautifully shaped and most are suitable for making this type of instrument. If only you can find them!

Cow's horn flutes, like ocarinas, belong to the vessel flute family. This means that the flute has no other openings and the air can only escape through the seven or eight finger holes and the window.

Preparing the horn
Cow's horns can generally be obtained from an abattoire. The upper part of the horn, which contains hair and bits of flesh, is cut off at right angles with a hacksaw, so that the cartilage is exposed. Cow's horns smell strongly and it is best to carry out this operation outdoors! In summer the horn can be left outside to dry. After a week or two, the cartilage dries and shrinks and can then be removed easily.
If the weather is cold or wet soak the horn for a while in hot water before removing the cartilage.
Wash the horn thoroughly in soap and water. Ensure that the inside wall is completely smooth and then rub it well with sewing machine oil or instrument oil.
Use a piece of bent wire to find where the horn becomes solid. Lay the wire along the outside of the horn. The last finger hole must be positioned just before the end of the wire (see illustration).

The window and windway
The window and windway are made in the same way as they are made in the bone flute, the only difference being that the windway is filed only in the stop and not in the bone. Both window and windway are situated on the underside of the flute. This allows saliva to escape – if saliva remains inside the flute, it will soon begin to sound out of tune.
Only fix the plaster stop in position with wood glue after all the finger holes have been bored, any bone dust has been removed and the inside wall is completely smooth.

The finger holes
The cow's horn flute has seven finger holes and a thumb hole. Hold the flute up to the lips, place the fingers on the horn and so determine the position of these holes. Bore them out and file them smooth.

Playing the cow's horn flute
This does not differ much from playing the elder and bone flutes. A fingering table is given for the basic scale of middle C.

A good example of a cow's horn flute. When making your own model, we advise you to place the window on the under side so saliva drains away better. In this model the window is on the upper side.

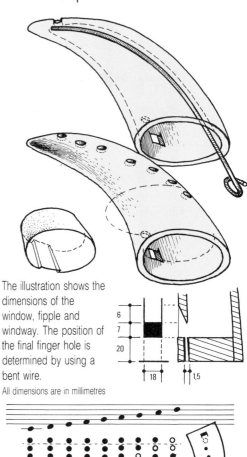

The illustration shows the dimensions of the window, fipple and windway. The position of the final finger hole is determined by using a bent wire.
All dimensions are in millimetres

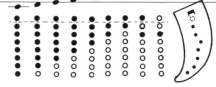

This table shows the fingering system for a cow's horn flute.

Clay flutes

Clay flutes can either be globular or straight. Globular flutes (vessel flutes) can be made in a wide variety of shapes. They are often made in the form of animals, particularly birds, but human figures are also found. From the earliest times until the Middle Ages, it was generally thought that playing an instrument was a form of witchcraft. People found it difficult to imagine that a melody could be produced by nothing but the breath. Tales such as 'The Pied Piper of Hamelen' and 'The Magic Flute' are good examples of this belief. In many Anglo-Saxon countries a type of flute, which had a specially designed funnel at one end, was placed on the roof. This produced a mysterious low moan when the wind blew and was intended to keep evil spirits away from the house. Even today, there are people who whistle in the dark when they are afraid! In some villages clay flutes were put in the crib in order to protect the baby.

Many of the clay flute variations date from early times, when the shapes served to strengthen their magical powers.

Clay flutes of every shape and size. These flutes are ideally suited to allow you to give your imagination free rein and can be decorated to your own taste and preference.

Making a vessel flute (ocarina)

Ordinary potters' clay is too oily and so it is best to use clay which contains chamotte powder or (if you do not have access to a ceramic oven) self-hardening hobby clay.

Knead the clay thoroughly into a ball of about 50 mm in diameter. Cut this ball exactly in half using a sharp knife and knead each half into a hollow hemisphere (B and C). The smoother and more uniform the inner walls of these hemispheres are, the more beautiful the tone of this finished flute will be. Rub your wetted finger over the edges of the two hemispheres to produce a slib and 'glue' them together (D).

Use a length of wood to flatten the hollow sphere slightly so that it is more or less oval in shape. Use the same piece of wood to press one side of the oval flat (E-G).

Aerophones

You can even make a flute with the aid of an eggshell and clay.

The illustration shows the various steps in the making of a vessel flute. You begin with a ball of clay, cut in half, from which you make a hollow, oval shape. The tools are two narrow metal strips sharpened into chisel form, a nail, a strip of wood and a hair dryer.

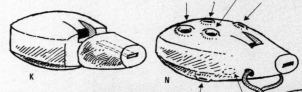

Dry this flattened side of the sphere with a hairdryer so that the clay is firmer and easier to work. A strip of metal, approx. 8 mm in width and sharpened to the shape of a paring chisel, is pushed through this flat side at an angle until the end touches the opposite inner wall (H.) The lip of the window is now cut sharply using a second paring chisel. The edge of the window must be very sharp, otherwise surface noise will arise. Now remove the metal strip and cut a hole under the lip with a sharp knife (I).

The mouthpiece is made by rolling a piece of clay into the form of a truncated cone. This cone must be slightly tapered. A narrow windway is made by pushing a sharp metal strip, which is of the same width as the window, through the mouthpiece so that the windway is in line with the upper lip of the window (J and K).

Push a large nail through the lower part of the mouthpiece to make a hole through which a cord can later be attached. Do this while the metal strip is still in place, or the pressure will tend to close the windway.

Four finger holes (K) must now be made in the upper side of the vessel and two thumb holes (L) in the underside. Make these in the positions where your fingers sit most naturally. Hold the mouthpiece against the vessel and check if it is now possible to play an entire octave (K). If not, then the finger holes must be enlarged. The larger the hole, the higher the pitch and in this way the vessel can be tuned. Remnants of clay inside the finger holes can be removed through the window.

The mouthpiece is attached to the vessel by slib – wetted clay – (M). Hold the mouthpiece against the vessel and blow through the windway. The pitch of the flute can be determined by varying the position of the mouthpiece in relation to the vessel. When you have found the right pitch, fix the two parts together.

Attach a small ring finger support (N) to the back of the vessel with slib. Now allow the flute to dry thoroughly or fire it in a ceramic oven at 1000° C. Before firing make sure that the flute is thoroughly dry, a day in the sun or on a radiator is sufficient. If moisture remains in the clay the flute can collapse – or even explode – while it is being fired. If you wish, you can paint or glaze the flute before firing.

Playing the vessel flute

In the illustration you can not only see how the flute should be tuned, but also the fingering which is necessary to obtain a particular pitch. In this flute there are two thumb holes on the underside. If all the holes

Hans Goddefroy demonstrates how a vessel flute must be played. When you are playing, you support the flute with the ring fingers.

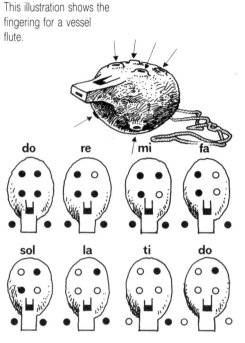

This illustration shows the fingering for a vessel flute.

do   re   mi   fa

sol   la   ti   do

are closed the lowest pitch, Do is obtained. For Re, the middle finger of the right hand is lifted; for Mi, the index finger; and so on. With a little practice, you will soon be able to play simple tunes on your clay flute.

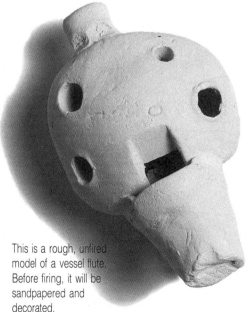

This is a rough, unfired model of a vessel flute. Before firing, it will be sandpapered and decorated.

An example of a home-made pipe flute. All you need to make this instrument are a wooden kitchen spoon, a knife, a nail and a small screwdriver. And clay, of course!

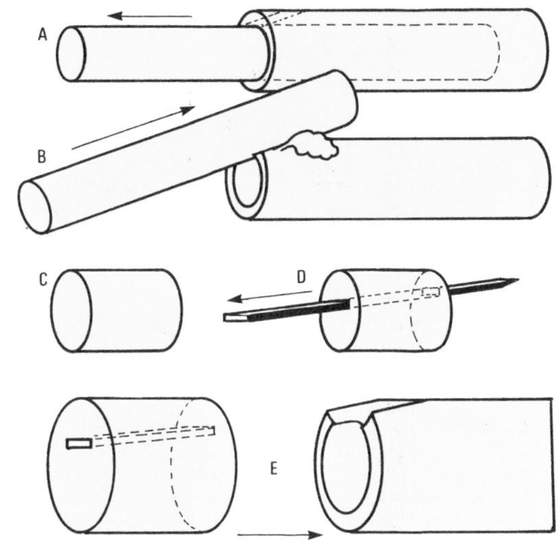

A

B

C

D

E

The step by step
diagram on the left
shows how to make a
pipe flute.

First determine the correct position of the mouthpiece – in the same way as for the vessel flute – and fix the two parts of the flute together (E) with wetted clay (slib).

One or more finger holes can be made with a nail. Allow the clay to dry thoroughly or bake it in an oven. The instrument can be painted in whatever way you choose.

Making a pipe flute

Self-hardening hobby clay is a handy material for making clay flutes because it does not need to be fired and therefore no oven is needed. Besides clay, you need only four tools to make this flute, a knife, a wooden kitchen spoon, a screwdriver and a nail.

The most primitive type of pipe flute is made as follows. Roll out a clay 'sausage' which has a diameter of about 20 mm. Smear the handle of the kitchen spoon with butter and push the clay 'sausage' over it (A). (The butter makes it easier for the clay to slide over the wood). The flute is closed at one end and the handle is therefore not pushed completely through the clay.

Harden the clay, using a hairdryer, so that the pipe can be easily removed from the handle of the spoon. Use the spoon handle to make an indentation, the window, in the pipe (B) – in primitive flutes surplus clay remnants are left 'in situ' but they can be removed if wished.

For the mouthpiece (C), roll a 'sausage' of clay about 30 mm long and the same diameter as the flute. Push a screwdriver through the clay from one end diagonally upwards in order to form a window. This should be at the level of the window (D). Cut off this end of the mouthpiece at right angles.

Playing the pipe flute

In this instrument, too, the fingering is important in the playing of simple tunes. This fingering depends on the number of finger holes you have made. Of course, it takes time before you acquire sufficient experience to play more complex melodies, but the results are well worth the effort!

This flute shows that there are endless possibilities in the designing and making of a vessel flute. The model shown here, made by Hans Goddefroy, consists of two flutes and can be played by two people at the same time.

The Pied Piper's flute

This flute, sometimes known as the fife, is a small transverse flute. This means that the blow hole is not at the end of the pipe but on the side. The flute is made in one piece and the end nearest the blow hole is usually stopped. Since time immemorial this type of flute has been used to play military music. It is easy to make and a variety of materials, such as elder wood or bamboo, thick-walled, hard plastic tubing or impact-resistant PVC tubing, can be used.

Making a Pied Piper's flute

This instrument can be made from various materials – elder wood, pvc (plastic), and so on. If you are using elder, you need a branch about 33 cm in length. This must first be dried and hollowed out in the manner described on page 15. If using some other material, you can begin immediately.

The blow hole and finger holes
The positions of the finger holes and blow hole are measured from the far end (mouth) of the tube (see illustration).

The blow hole always has a diameter of 8.5 mm – no matter what the size or the length of the pipe. Over the years, the round blow hole has been replaced by an oval one as this improves the quality of the sound. Other developments in flute building – by the famous instrument maker, Theobald Böhm – include more angular holes and the use of metal for the body instead of wood.

After the blow hole has been bored, the inner edge is opened up slightly (see the illustration far right) with a whittling knife (see: Tools).

In practice, it is much easier to make small 'starter holes' (using a sharp-pointed instrument such as an awl) before you begin to bore. This prevents the drill point from slipping.

The six finger holes are bored in the pipe, following the schema in the illustration at bottom right, using a slow-speed drill. Begin with a small hole and enlarge it in 0.5 mm stages – this helps prevent the wood splitting. Burrs and splinters of wood inside the pipe must be carefully removed using a bottle brush or a whittling knife. The Pied Piper's flute is tuned in the same way as the elder flute (See: page 16).

The stop
Finally a cork stop is inserted 3 mm from the blow hole. If the distance between the stop and the blow hole is greater than 3 mm the pitch is lowered. If it is less than 3 mm the pitch is raised.

Above left: A colored engraving dating from the last century, showing a musician playing this type of flute.

The fingering table (right) for this type of flute. It is the same as that for the elder flute.

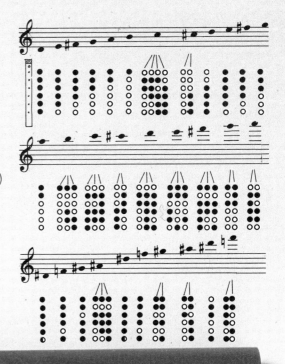

Playing the Pied Piper's flute
It takes a great deal of patience to learn to play this instrument. This is because it is played transversely – the mouthpiece is on the side – and the window is formed, as it were, by the mouth and the blow hole together.

Hold the flute horizontally at right angles to the mouth. It is held by the thumbs, the little finger of the right hand and the lower lip. The right hand covers the three holes at the end of the flute and the left hand the three nearest the blow hole. Do not blow directly into the blow hole but against the upper edge. If you blow gently, the air in the flute will vibrate. Place your lower lip against the underside of the blow hole and blow against the upper edge, with the lips almost closed, and at the same time 'roll' the flute very slightly.

When you have discovered the correct playing position and can create a lovely rounded tone, you can concentrate on the fingering. You can then learn the scales and will soon be playing simple tunes!

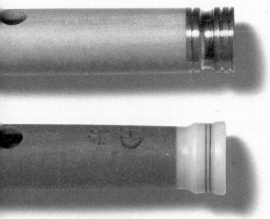

On this page you can see four examples of this type of flute. The top one is made of epramid, a synthetic material. The others are professionally made examples and are of wood with bone and brass fittings.

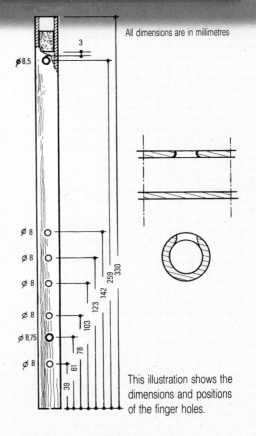

All dimensions are in millimetres

This illustration shows the dimensions and positions of the finger holes.

The multiple flute

Music for several flutes has existed as long as the instrument itself. Sometimes a single musician played a number of flutes and in some cultures this led to the invention of the multiple flute. There are many variations. Some multiple flutes have a single mouthpiece. Others, such as panpipes, have several flutes side by side, although they do not have finger holes.

Making a multiple flute

A multiple flute can be made from lean clay or clay to which chamotte powder has been added. This material must be fired and you therefore need an oven in which the flute can be heated to a temperature of approximately 1000°C.

If you do not own (or have access to) such an oven then use self-hardening hobby clay. To construct a multiple flute, you actually begin by making three pipe flutes. Do this, following the instructions under 'Making a pipe flute' on page 21. Bear in mind that the basic pitches – the fundamentals – of the three flutes must be in tune with each other. This is achieved by constructing the flutes in different lengths. Choose three basic pitches which sound good together – C, F and G, for example. In order to make a multiple flute from these three pipe flutes you require a 'windcap'. This is simply a device which allows you to play the three flutes through a single windway.

Take a piece of clay and roll it out into a flat strip approximately 4 mm in thickness. This strip must be long enough to fit round the three mouthpieces when placed together (see illustration). As shown in the illustration, the flutes can be positioned in different ways. You can even use more than three flutes – as long as you possess a powerful pair of lungs! When you have chosen the position of the flutes, flatten them slightly on the sides where they will be joined and fix them together with slib. Mount the strip around the mouthpieces with slib.

Now make a 'lid' which has a mouthpiece and blow hole (see illustration) and attach it over the open end. Finally use a nail to make holes for the various pitches in one of the outer flutes (see the illustration). The flute is tuned by ear.

Playing the multiple flute

Because you are blowing into the flutes via the windcap, all that is necessary to play a tune is to vary the pitch by means of the fingering. The fingering depends on the number of holes you have made. It is quite possible, for example, to use the middle flute as a bourdon and produce a constant basic pitch. You can also 'eliminate' one or more flutes by closing off the windows.

24

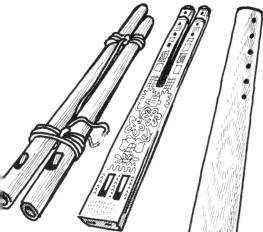

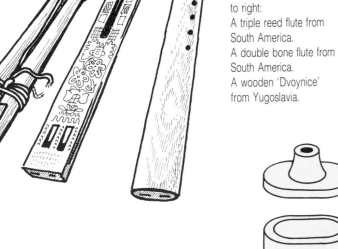

Left: The illustration shows examples of multiple flutes. From left to right:
A triple reed flute from South America.
A double bone flute from South America.
A wooden 'Dvoynice' from Yugoslavia.

A double wooden flute from Rumania.

Below: The illustration shows how you can make a multiple flute out of clay.

To do this you need a wooden kitchen spoon, a knife, a small screw-driver, clay and a nail. This multiple flute consists of a combination of three pipe flutes with a cap forming a single windway.

Far right: a variation made from one piece of clay. Make sure the wind cap fits tightly over the mouthpieces.

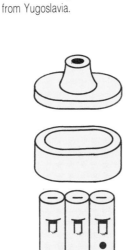

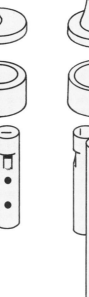

A hand-made model of a multiple flute. This is made from lean clay with chamotte powder.

Two flutes provide the basic tone while the melody can be played on the third. The pitch can be altered by covering the windows with the fingers.

Pan, an ancient Greek god, playing the panpipes. According to legend. Pan was in love with a nymph who, fleeing from his attentions, was turned into a reed by a protective deity. Pan made a flute out of this reed and played on it in order to console himself.

Two examples of an organ flute. In contrast to the panpipes, this flute has mouthpieces which make it much easier to play. (see p. 28).

26

The organ flute

The organ flute, or 'panpipes with mouthpiece', is a variation of ordinary panpipes. Panpipes consist of a 'bundle' of flutes without mouthpieces. These flutes do not have fingerholes and the ends are usually stopped. According to legend this instrument was invented by the Greek god, Pan. Because panpipes are very difficult to play, a variation which does have mouthpieces — the organ flute — has been created.

Making an organ flute

Traditonally, panpipes are made from reed because the nymph fleeing from the besotted god Pan was herself turned into a reed. Pan cut his pipes from this reed and, according to legend, played them ever afterwards.

The organ flute described here is made from a hardwood such as meranti or mahogany, and consists of six separate straight-sided pipes glued together. The longest pipe is 180 mm, the next 170 mm, and so on to the shortest, which is 130 mm.

Saw the six lengths from a piece of wood of cross-section 20 × 20 mm. Mount each length in an electric drill stand. Set the machine at its lowest speed and carefully bore them out, using a long drill bit 10 mm in diameter. Bevel the edges of each piece with a rasp or sandpaper. Glue them together with wood glue so that both the ends and upper sides form a flat surface (see photograph).

The mouthpieces

There are two ways to make the mouthpieces. Method A: The windows are cut out following illustration A, using a tenon saw, a chisel and a file. Notice how the windows increase in size as the flutes increase in length. When you have cut the windows, clean and smooth the edges thoroughly with sandpaper. Take a length of dowel 10 mm in diameter (the same material as the pipes) and cut six lengths of 20 mm. Make one side of each piece flat by filing it down or by rubbing it across a piece of coarse sandpaper. These pieces are now glued into the ends of the pipes to form the mouthpieces. Ensure that the flat side is uppermost (this forms the windway) and that each plug is inserted up to the beginning of the window. The underside of the mouthpieces can now be cut off diagonally (see illustration), but this is not absolutely necessary.

Method B: The ends of the pipes must be absolutely level – if necessary saw or file off any protruding wood. Saw off the last 20 mm of the pipes – part of this section will later be used to make the mouthpieces. Now cut the windows. Notice that the upper line is at an angle because the size of the windows increases as the length of the pipe increases. Glue a diagonally cut strip of wood along the ends of the pipes (This is the shaded section in illustration B). The upper part of the mouthpieces will be glued to this. Saw transversely in half the 20 mm strip which you cut off in the first stage. Clean out the windways with a file and glue on top of the diagonally-cut wooden strip.

The stops
The ends of the six pipes must be stopped. Use the same 10 mm diameter dowel as used for the mouthpiece plugs. The pipes can be tuned by varying the position of the stops. Adjust each stop until you achieve the correct pitch, then glue it in position and cut off any surplus. Finally, sandpaper the instrument thoroughly, remove any traces of glue and varnish it.

Playing the organ flute
In contrast to the panpipes, the organ flute is held straight out from the mouth. Its advantage is that once it has been tuned it is not at all difficult to play. Of course, you can make an organ flute with more than six pipes – in fact the number of pipes is limited only by the difficulty in handling multiple-pipe instruments.

Above: Three young Argentinians playing self-made panpipes. This instrument is very common in South America. The models on which they are playing have a double row of pipes.

The illustration on the right contains the information necessary for you to make your own organ flute. Two methods of making the mouthpiece are shown.

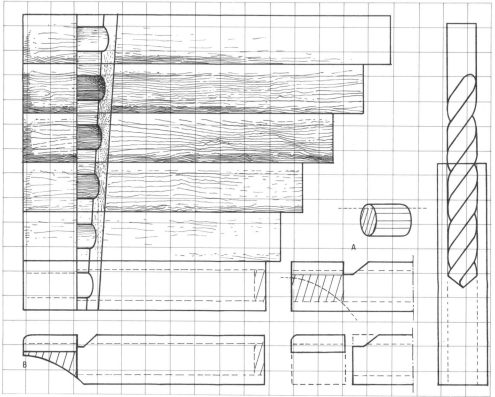

The reed flute

The reed flute is not actually a flute at all but a clarinet, because the sound is created by a vibrating reed and not by blowing against the lip of a window (end-blown flutes) or across a blow hole (side-blown flutes). This folk clarinet originated in ancient Egypt and from there spread through North Africa and Europe. These reed flutes are distinguished because the air is made to vibrate by a single reed or tongue which is cut into a cylindrical tube. The lips close over the flute behind the reed.

A good example of a home-made reed flute. This instrument is easy to make yet has a very impressive and surprising sound.

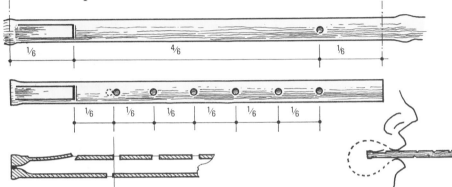

The illustration shows the proportions of the reed and finger holes of this simple reed flute. Notice that in the playing position, the lips are closed over the reed which is entirely inside the mouth.

Preparing the reed

A length of reed (cane or bamboo can also be used) is used to make this instrument. This can still be found growing naturally but can be bought at a garden center. Choose a straight length and cut off the node at one end. Clean out the inside using a bottle brush or something similar. Should there be an opening at the node end, close it with sealing wax.

The reed itself

Divide the length of the flute into six equal parts (see illustration). A 'V-shaped' notch is cut at one-sixth distance from the closed end of the pipe. The best tool for this is a sharp hobby knife. Cut the sides of the reed to about 10 mm from the end of the tube. Do not cut at right angles to the center but diagonally. This ensures that the reed is free to move and does not stick when blown or when it is damp. This is very important and you are advised to study the illustration carefully before you begin. The reed can be strengthened by wrapping cotton or some other strong thread around the end of the flute and coating this with wax. If the reed in thinned or bent upwards it will vibrate when you blow against it.

If the reed is thinned at the end where the notch is, it will produce a higher pitch. If, on the other hand, it is thinned at its foot, the pitch will be lower. The reed is thinned on its upper side, using a sharp hobby knife or a flat file.

If the reed sticks, there may be burrs inside the tube. Remove these. If the reed still sticks, a hair inserted between it and the pipe will probably help.

The finger holes

The last finger hole is situated at a distance of one-sixth of the total length from the end of the flute (see illustration). The hole is burned in the flute with a red-hot awl.

The distance between the last finger hole and the notch is again divided by six and the 2nd, 3rd, 4th and 5th finger holes are burned. The 1st hole, however, is moved 3 mm nearer to the 2nd, while the thumb hole on the underside is placed 3 mm nearer to the reed (see illustration).

The larger the hole, the higher the pitch. It is easier to enlarge a hole than it is to make it smaller, and you are therefore advised to begin by burning small holes and enlarging them as necessary.

Playing

You can practice the blowing technique for the reed flute with the aid of a straw and a glass of water. When blowing, breathe through your nose. In this way you are able to produce a constant sound.

The fingering table for the reed flute, also sometimes known as a 'penny whistle'.

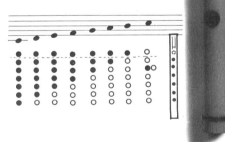

Playing the reed flute

To play this instrument, the mouthpiece must be taken completely inside the mouth while blowing. The reed will vibrate and produce a lovely full, warm tone. Melodies can be played by opening and closing the finger holes. The table above shows the required fingering for the key of middle C.

An Indian snake charmer, playing his 'tiktiri' – a double clarinet – an instrument which is found throughout the Indian sub-continent. The tiktiri consists of two reed flutes which are mounted into a gourd. This acts both as the mouth pipe and the air reservoir.

Three examples of multiple reed flutes from various cultures.

30

The double reed flute

The multiple reed flute was developed even earlier than the basic multiple flute. Rather than a number of musicians playing a number of flutes, two-, three-, and four-fold reed flutes were created. These instruments are widely used, particularly in Arabic countries.

A multiple reed flute usually consists of a melody pipe (called the chanter) and a base pipe (called the drone or bourdon).

Mechel Goddefroy shows how to play the double reed flute.

The separate mouthpiece

The melody pipe of a double reed flute is made in the same way as a single reed flute but, as a variation, a smaller mouthpiece can be made from another piece of reed. The advantage of a separate mouthpiece is that the reed dries more quickly.

For the mouthpiece, select a length of reed which fits exactly inside the melody pipe. Taper the end of the reed slightly in order to ensure a good fit. The nodes must be cut off the pipe so the reed can be pushed in.

In order to determine the positions of the finger holes, the mouthpiece must first be inserted into the pipe. The total length of the pipe, including the reed, is divided into six. The last finger hole is situated at one-sixth from the end of the pipe, while the notch in

the reed is one-sixth from the end where the mouth is (see illustration). The distance between the notch and the last finger hole is again divided by six, as in the single reed flute, and the finger holes burned out. Make the reed according to the instructions on page 29.

It is better to make narrow mouthpieces, particularly when a multiple folk clarinet consists of more than two melody and bourdon pipes. The mouthpiece, like the end of the pipe, is strengthened with thread. The different parts of the flute are also fixed together with thread (see illustration).

A double reed flute with a melody pipe and a bass pipe (bourdon). The bourdon is fitted with a metal funnel ('mouth horn') which enhances the sound.

The bourdon pipe

The bourdon pipe is a reed flute without finger holes. The mouthpiece and the pipe are made in the same way as they are in the melody pipe. The longer the bourdon pipe, the lower the pitch. The bourdon pipe can be built up from a number of pipes, so creating variations in the sound produced. The bass sound of the bourdon pipe can be emphasized by attaching a funnel to the end of the pipe. This funnel can easily be made from tin or copper (see illustration) and can also be attached to the pipe by thread.

The double pipe

The two pipes are finally attached together by means of stiff thread. The melody pipe should be on the left and the bourbon on the right. When playing the multiple reed flute, the lips must be placed over both reeds.

Playing the multiple reed flute

When the multiple reed flute is played, the bourdon pipe produces a constant accompanying tone. Tunes can be played on the melody pipe, using the fingering described for the reed flute on page 29.

The illustration shows the proportions of the double reed flute. The flute differs from a single reed flute in that the reeds are contained in separate mouthpieces, so that the position of the finger holes deviates slightly. The letters A, B and C refer to the way in which the pipes are assembled. The trumpet-like end piece can be made from thin sheets of copper or tin soldered at the edges.

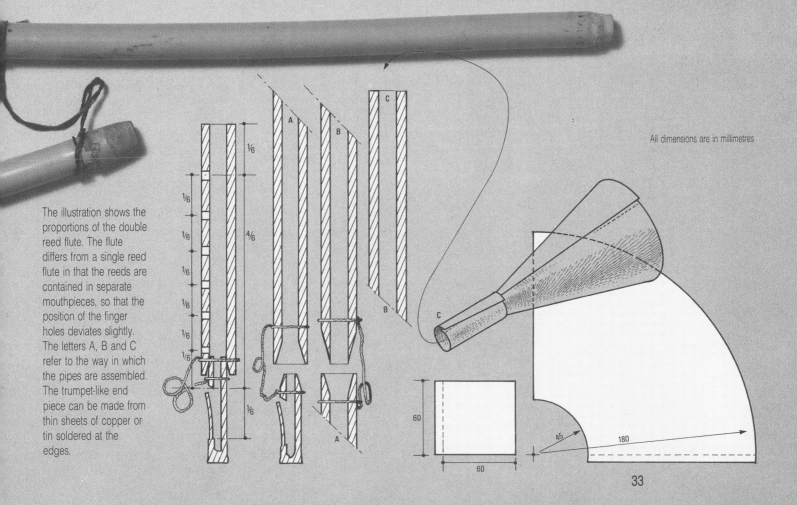

All dimensions are in millimetres

33

The bagpipes

Most people immediately associate the bagpipes with Scotland. This instrument, however, has been played in dozens of different forms throughout Europe, Asia and Africa since Roman times.

The sound produced by the bagpipes or, for example, the Arghûl, Zummâra, Launeddas, Musette or Uilleann Pipes, is characterized by its uninterrupted nasal quality. This is because, besides the melody pipe (the chanter), one of more bass pipes (bourdons) can be heard. These pipes are connected to a single air reservoir – the bag – which is filled by blowing air through the mouth pipe. When the piper is not actually blowing, he forces air out of this bag and through the pipes, so producing a continuous sound.

Bagpipes exist in all shapes and varieties. The simplest form consists of a bag, a mouth pipe, a melody pipe or chanter and a bass pipe or bourdon.

The three pipes are made of elder wood and the reeds from elder or cane. When making a set of bagpipes, treat the wood in the same way as for the elder flute (see: page 15). Make sure it is thoroughly dry and that the internal walls are smooth. In making the bagpipes described in this chapter, the natural shape of the wood is adhered to and therefore a lathe is not used. The branches must be selected very carefully and their dimensions should be as close as possible to those given. Branches can be brought to roughly the correct size with the aid of a rasp. In fact, the pipes illustrated on page 36 were made using nothing but a rasp and sandpaper!

The bag

The bag of a set of bagpipes can consist of a cow's bladder, but it is a fairly simple matter to make a leather bag using a supple piece of calf's skin.

An example of Turkish bagpipes made from a goatskin turned inside out and furnished with a double chanter.

A musical duo in Mallorca, Spain. One man is playing the 'xerimies', a set of bagpipes. The other is playing a 'flogal', a flute for one hand.

Aerophones

The bagpipes illustrated here were made by the Belgian, Kris Geysens. The pipes are made of elder and are so beautifully worked with a rasp and sandpaper that one has the impression that they were turned on a lathe. A good example of how a self-made instrument can have a character of its own.

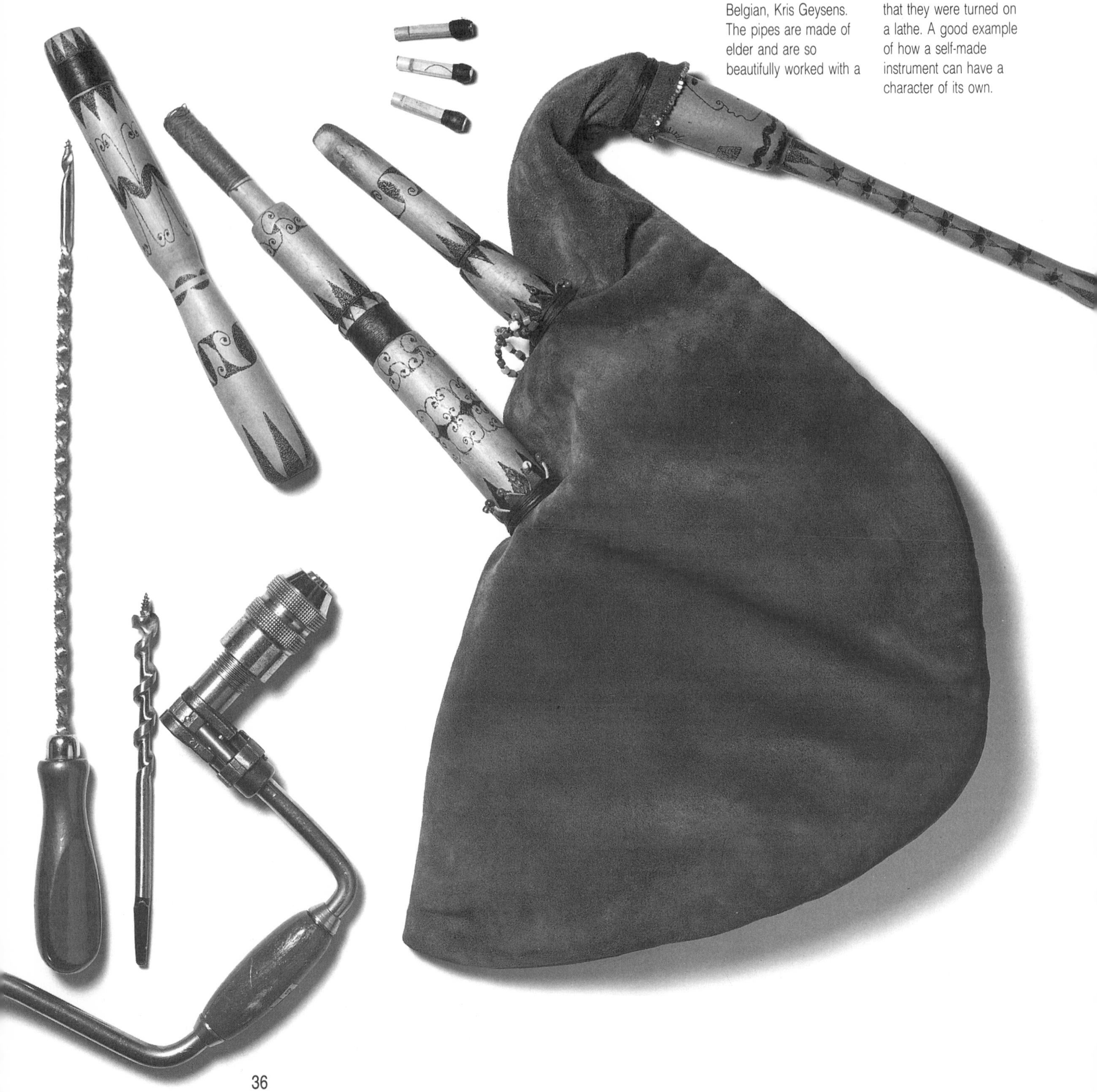

Use the grid to enlarge the pattern of the bag to the size you require and cut it out. Lay the pattern on a double-folded piece of leather and cut out the bag. The seams can be stitched on almost any household sewing machine.

Make the seam airtight by glueing a strip of leather over the seam with special leather adhesive. (Don't forget to degrease the leather with acetone before you begin!). Now turn the bag inside out so that seam and strip are on the inside.

The bag can be made airtight by treating it with an anti-condensation product, made as follows: mix 25 gm cabinetmaker's glue with 10 cl water and heat in a 'bain-marie'. Add 10 cl glycerine oil and a tablespoon salicylic acid. Mix thoroughly and, while warm, pour it into the bag. After a few minutes, pour out the mixture and drain the bag. The narrow end of the bag remains open and the two holes for the chanter and bourdon pipes are cut in the form of a star, using a sharp knife, in the positions indicated.

The chanter

The chanter (top center, right) consists of a stock, a melody pipe and a reed. The stock is made from a piece of elder wood which must be bored to size (16 mm). It is a little wider towards the end which fits into the bag and the inside must be very smooth. Make a deep V-shaped notch close to the end of the stock. This notch is fitted in the narrow opening of the bag (A) as shown in the illustration below. The joint is strengthened with wax, pitch or thread.

The elder wood melody pipe is made in the same way as the elder flute – but without a window and windway.
Select a piece of wood which has an internal diameter of about 8 mm and walls 4 mm in thickness.
Remove the pith and leave the wood to dry for a few weeks. Clean and smooth the inner wall and bore the finger holes as indicated in the illustration, using a red-hot awl.
Begin with small holes and, if necessary, enlarge them. Smooth the holes and the ends of the pipe with sandpaper.
A free reed – which is made in exactly the same way as the reed for the double reed flute – is fitted in the end of the melody pipe (A, illustration right).

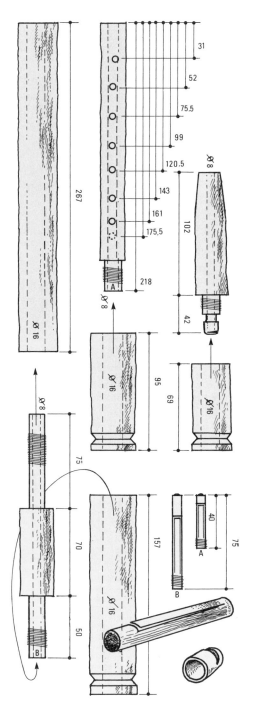

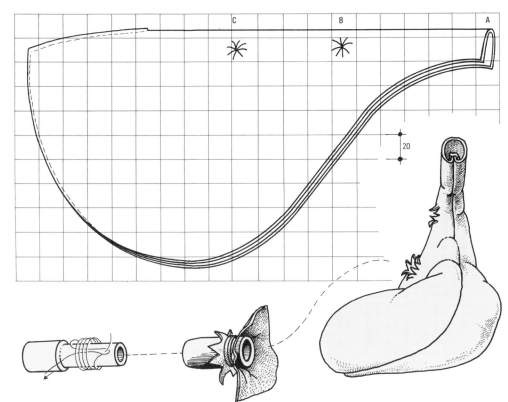

In this illustration you can see all the various parts of the bagpipes. Notice in particular how the one way valve in the mouth pipe must be fixed in the holder. The grid beneath the sack makes it possible to enlarge the pattern precisely to size.

All dimensions are in millimetres

37

If the reed does not fit snugly, wrap thread around the end or enlarge the melody pipe slightly.

Also wrap thread round the base of the melody pipe so that it fits tightly when mounted into the stock.

The mouth pipe
The mouth pipe (far right) consists of two parts – the stock and the mouth pipe itself – and is attached to the bag via the hole nearest the chanter (B). The stock is made in the same way as that of the chanter. The mouth pipe must fit tightly into the stock – wrap thread round to ensure a good fit.

A one-way valve is inserted in the end of the mouth pipe in order to prevent the bag losing air when the player is not blowing. This valve should actually consist of a piece of leather but it is simpler to use a plastic cap. After a while leather becomes hard and then it does not close properly. The plastic cap is cut almost completely through close to the end to form a flexible flap. A length of plastic or copper tubing is fitted into the mouth pipe and the valve glued into it. Ensure that the internal diameter of the stock is larger than that of the valve (see illustration)!

The bourdon pipe
The bourdon pipe (bottom center and left in the illustration right) is attached to the bag through the remaining hole (C). The middle section of this pipe consists of a piece of hollow elder in which a copper tube is inserted. This tube is wrapped with thread at both ends and then mounted in the stock and the top part of the pipe (see illustration).

A precise fit is essential. You must also ensure that the wider end of the elder wood center section is towards the end of the pipe and the narrower end towards of the bag. The third section of the bourdon pipe is made in the same way as that for the double reed flute. The second reed is fitted into the copper tube (B, illustration right). In order to make it fit tightly, wrap thread around it and smear it with wax.

The joints where the different parts of the pipes fit together must be airtight. To achieve this, the threads are smeared with a mixture

Three examples of sets of bagpipes. From left to right: Arabic, Russian an Polish bagpipes, the latter furnished with a pair of bellows.

of 50% grease and 50% wax. This mixture is heated in a bain marie – a pan which is placed in another pan containing hot water – and brushed into the thread. In places where the different parts must be able to slide freely, as in the bourdon pipe, the threads are additionally treated with paraffin or vaseline.

Playing the bagpipes
Two fingerings are shown – one half-closed, one open. By practicing these fingerings you will soon learn to play a scale. The difficult thing in playing the bagpipes is to find the right balance between the air entering, and the air leaving, the bag. The pressure exerted must be in rhythm with the breathing pattern so that there is a constant stream of air through the chanter and the bourdon. To put it another way – when you breathe in, increase the pressure on the bag.

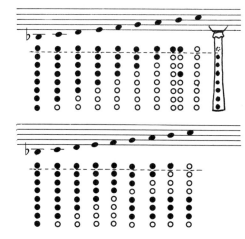

This table gives both open (above) and half-closed (below) methods of fingering.

Herman Dewit, playing a self-made set of bagpipes against the background of a Flemish landscape.

Primitive trumpets

In primitive trumpets the sound is produced by the vibration of the player's lips. This is also the manner in which the sound is produced in horns. Horns, however, tend to be curved and conical, whereas trumpets are usually straight and cylindrical. Trumpets have existed all over the world for thousands of years and, like flutes, are often associated with ritual and magic. The brass trumpet, the so-called 'orchestral trumpet', appeared during the course of the eighteenth century.

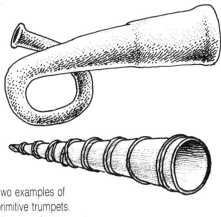

Two examples of primitive trumpets. Above, a clay trumpet from Peru. Below, a wooden trumpet from Hungary.

Rubber hose and funnel

A very simple trumpet can be made from a length of rubber hose, a plastic funnel and a mouthpiece of bamboo or elder wood. The hose can vary in length between 30 cm and 150 cm. A funnel, which acts a sounding beaker, is pushed into one end of the hose. This funnel can either be glued in position or tied tightly in place with a length of strong thread. For the mouthpiece you need a piece of elder wood, 6 cm long, which fits tightly over the end of the hose. Make sure the wood is thoroughly dry. The mouthpiece can be cut at right angles and the edges rounded off or cut diagonally, as in the photograph.

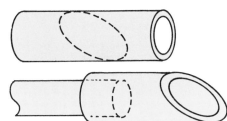

One method of making a mouthpiece from elder wood. This can be used for your self-made trumpet.

A length of elder is hollowed out and cut diagonally. The tube is glued into the mouthpiece.

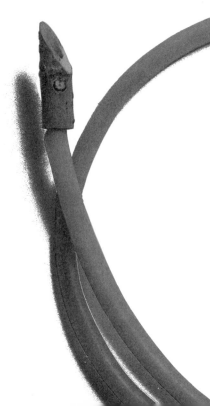

Playing the primitive trumpet

This instrument is played by placing the pursed lips against the mouthpiece and forcing air through them. In theory, a series of basic notes can be played on this trumpet, but a great deal depends on the lip technique of the player. A good player, who has experience, will be able to produce surprisingly beautiful sounds from this instrument. An extra effect can be produced by swinging the trumpet around in a circle while playing it.

A primitive trumpet made from a length of garden hose, a funnel and an elder wood mouthpiece. A resounding blast can be made by swinging the funnel round when playing.

39

Hans Goddefroy shows
how to play a self-made
wooden horn. This is not
easy because the notes
are formed by pressing
the mouth against the
mouthpiece while at the
same time forcing air
between the lips.

40

Horns

In horns the sound is produced in the same way as it is produced in trumpets, namely by causing air to vibrate between the lips. In contrast to a trumpet, a horn has a curved, conical shape. The simplest types consist of an animal horn or a large sea shell. Few melodies can be played on most primitive horns, even though some of them have finger holes.

In some parts of Europe – Twente in the Netherlands, for example – there is a long tradition of mid-winter horn blowing. Every conceivable type of horn – cow's horns, horns made of old cans, wood or bronze horns between one and two metres in length – are used in these festivals.

Two examples of the horn. The top one is made from the horn of an Indian cow and has a hollowed mouthpiece. In the horn below, a branch is hollowed out and the two parts held together with flexible thin strips of wood. The mouthpiece is a piece of diagonally cut elder wood.

Making a horn

A branch from a beech, alder or willow tree is used to make this horn. Choose a branch which is slightly curved. The diameter of the narrower end should be 30 to 40 mm and that of the broader end 70 to 80 mm. The length of the branch can vary.

Use an ordinary handsaw to saw the branch in half lengthwise. Remove the pith, using a gouge. When you have done this, the wall should be about 10 mm in thickness. Sandpaper the inner walls until they are very smooth. Now use water-resistant wood glue to glue the two halves back together. Do this immediately so that the wood has no chance to dry out and warp or twist.

41

To strengthen the horn, wrap split reed every 100 mm along its length and glue it in position. Then pour a little oil into the horn so that the whole of the inner wall is covered. The mouthpiece consists of a length of hollowed-out elder wood which fits exactly into the narrower end of the horn. This is pushed into the horn and fixed in place with split reed. As with the trumpet, you can choose a mouthpiece cut at right angles or one cut diagonally. The inner edges of a right-angled mouthpiece must be rounded off (see the illustration).

How a diagonally-cut mouthpiece is made is described on page 39. Remember that the internal diameter of the mouthpiece should not be greater than about 8 mm.

Playing the horn

Sound is also produced in this instrument by pressing the pursed lips against the mouthpiece and blowing through them. The position of the lips also determines the pitch.

Before playing, steep the horn in water for a while. It is best to play the instrument while it is soaking wet because the seams are then completely closed.

The two series of notes on the right can be played on this horn.

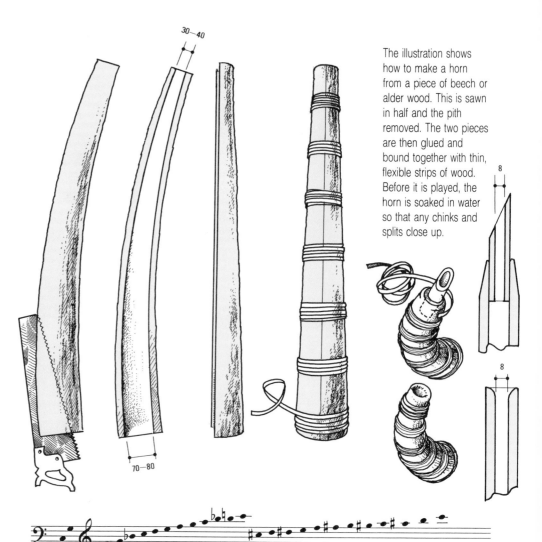

The illustration shows how to make a horn from a piece of beech or alder wood. This is sawn in half and the pith removed. The two pieces are then glued and bound together with thin, flexible strips of wood. Before it is played, the horn is soaked in water so that any chinks and splits close up.

After a great deal of practise, you will be able to play these scales on your horn.

Two examples of horns which can be made from actual horns! The top one is an antelope horn, the bottom one a water-buffalo horn.

Playing a self-made horn. This horn was built by Gerrit van den Dries and it is encased in a synthetic material, which seals any chinks or splits.

Idiophones

Idiophones are musical instruments which are made from resonant materials and although they can be played in many ways most idiophones are basically rhythm instruments.

This group of instruments includes – among others – rattles, bells, gongs, jingles, rasps, musical bottles and jars, sansas, steel drums, xylophones, cymbals, clappers and castanets. The very first idiophone was undoubtedly a simple stone which was beaten rhythmically against another stone, or perhaps a stick which was struck against a tree or a hollowed tree trunk.

Idiophones, particularly the basic rhythm instruments, can be extremely simple – like the original stones and sticks. More complex instruments, such as steel drums and xylophones, can be used to produce melodic sounds and demand greater skill from the player.

The best-known idiophone consists of two tablespoons which are struck together like clap sticks.

Children in West Java playing the 'anklung', a very refined rattle made of bamboo.
Precisely tuned bamboo pipes are moved up and down, producing a most pleasant sound as they strike the edges of the instrument.

Idiophones

The different tone colours and pitches of the musical instruments of the idiophone family are created by the differences in material and the differences in the way in which they are played – stamping, shaking, scraping, plucking, and so on.

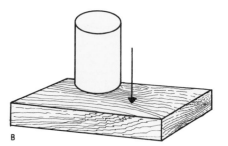

Stamping
Stamping idiophones are instruments in which the sound is created by banging them on the ground or other hard surface.
Examples include sticks, tubes and even tap dancing shoes. (A)

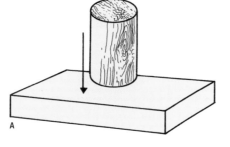

Stamped
In stamped idiophones the sound is produced by the surface on which the stamping takes place. Stamped pits and boards are good examples. It is possible to have a combination of both stamped and stamping idiophones. (B)

Shaken
In some idiophones – rattles and jingles, for example – the sound is produced by shaking the instrument. These idiophones are made from many different materials and in a wide variety of styles. (C)

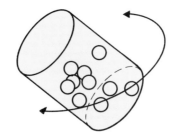

Percussion
Percussion idiophones, or struck idiophones, produce a sound when they are struck with a stick or some similar instrument. Xylophones and gongs are good examples. (D)

Concussion
Concussion idiophones, such as cymbals and clappers, make sounds when two similar parts are struck together. (E)

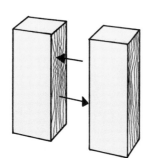

Friction
In friction idiophones the sound is produced by rubbing. This can occur, for example, when a wetted finger is rubbed along the rim of a glass or when two objects are rubbed against each other, as in the musical saw. (F)

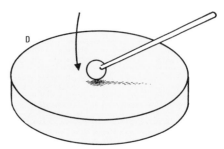

Scraped
These idiophones have a notched or ridged surface over which a stick or some similar instrument is scraped. Examples are notched sticks, cog rattles and washboards. (G)

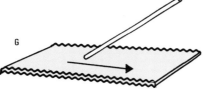

Plucked
Plucked idiophones have one or more flexible tongues attached to a frame. The sound is created by plucking these tongues. Good examples are sansas and Jew's harps. (H)

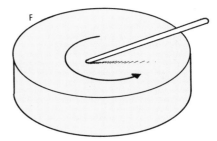

Rattles

In many countries a rattle is probably the very first musical instrument with which people become acquainted! Almost every baby has a rattle of some sort – although few, perhaps, go on to build musical carreers on these simple idiophones!

This is a pity, because for thousands of years rattles in one form or another have been used as accompanying and rhythmical instruments in cultures in every corner of the world.

Rattles can be made from all kinds of materials – wood, clay, animal skins, dried fruits, horn, bamboo, bronze, tin and ivory. The most simple rattles are dried gourds or pumpkins filled with seeds, but tin cans filled with dried peas work just as well.

Two examples of the sistrum. The top one has a rounded head which can be used as a drumstick.

Sistrum

A sistrum is a rattle in which the sound is made by jingling metal disks. Examples survive from ancient Egypt and Pompeii, among other places. There are all sorts of variations of this type of rattle.

Maple is an ideal wood from which to make the handle of a sistrum. The shape of the handle is drawn on a piece of wood, as indicated in the illustration, cut out with a fretsaw (or an electric jigsaw) and then thoroughly sandpapered. The handle can be varnished and decorated to your own taste.

The disks are cut or sawn from a sheet of hard bronze of approximately 1 mm thick. Drill a hole through the center of each disk. The two disks which are mounted on the one nail must differ slightly in size so that they touch over as large an area as possible. The disks are rounded by tapping them with a round-headed hammer. This process also hardens the surface of the disks so that the sound is pure and permanent.

Note: other materials can be used to make the disks, but this may be to the detriment of the sound. The disks are mounted on the handle with an ornamental nail or a wood screw.

This illustration shows the shape of a self-made sistrum. The grid makes it possible to enlarge the instrument to any size you wish. The disks can be beaten hollow using a round-headed hammer.

A self-made sistrum or rattle. Similar instruments have been found in excavations in Egypt and Pompeii, among other places.

Playing a rattle
A rattle is a rhythmical accompanying instrument and the disks jingle when the rattle is shaken. The rattle can also be used to strike a hard surface, your hand or thigh or even a drum.

47

The rinkelbom

When making a rinkelbom you can allow your imagination free rein. Anything that makes enough noise can by attached to this instrument! In Europe, at Carnival and other folk festivals, it is taken out of the store cupboard, dusted down, and used as a rhythm instrument. It is an ideal accompaniment for folk music ensembles and dance bands.

Anything that makes a noise!
An ordinary broomstick or the handle of a garden spade can be used for the neck of your rinkelbom. A large cookie tin forms the soundbox and this is attached to the neck with U-shaped bolts. The 'strings' are a single length of 2 mm steel wire, doubled in two, and attached to the neck as shown in the illustration on the right.

The rinkelbom is an instrument in which you can allow your imagination to run riot, for anything that makes a noise can be attached to it! A tambourine, which costs only a few dollars but which you can easily make yourself (see page 81), can be mounted on the end of the neck. Rattles, bells, strings of metal disks, small cans of seeds or nuts, flattened metal ashtrays or pan lids – as already stated above, anything that makes a noise can be added to the basic rinkelbom!

The illustration at bottom right also shows how you can even use wrought-iron shapes to decorate the neck.

Another possibility is to carve a series of notches along part of the underside of the neck. A striking musical accompaniment can be created by alternately scraping a stick along the notches and striking the strings, tambourine and cookie tin.

Scraping, shaking and stamping
Playing the rinkelbom is a combination of all the techniques for playing idiophones – stamping, shaking, scraping, friction and percussion methods are all used.
As a 'bow' you can use a simple hardwood stick or make a notched stick as described on page 61.

A festive variation of the rinkelbom, used at Carnival in the south of the Netherlands.

A self-made rinkelbom in which a cookie tin is used as the sound box and metal ashtrays as rattles.

Similar to the rinkelbom is the 'devil's instrument'. This has a devil's head whose eyes light up when the instrument is struck against the ground. An electrical contact is fixed to the end of the stick. The battery is in the cookie tin and wires run along the back of the stick. The 'eyes' are small light bulbs.

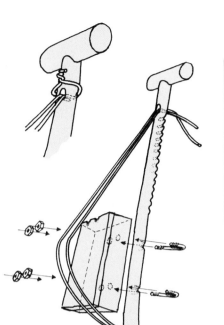

The illustration shows how the rinkelbom is assembled. The handle of a garden spade serves as the neck and the cookie tin is then bolted to it.

Two variations of the rinkelbom.

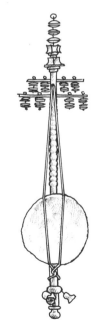

Jingles

'Jingles' is a general term used for a wide variety of small objects which, in one way or another, can be attached to the clothing or the body. Sound is created by rhythmical body movements.

In many cultures, dancers use jingles to form their own accompaniment. Warriors also used jingles in order to frighten the enemy when attacking. Examples of jingles are leather ankle bands, necklaces and belts, or even complete items of clothing to which bells, clappers, metal disks and rattles are attached. The 'rinkelbom rule' also applies here – anything that makes a noise makes a suitable jingle! The model below is made from a leather strap to which clowns' bells have been attached. To prevent chafing your skin while

playing, it is a good idea to wear the jingle over a glove or thick sock. You can also glue a soft material (foam rubber, for example) to the inside of the leather.

Below: An Indian princess bedecked from top to toe in jingles.

A jingle in the form of an ankle band. This was made from clown's bells and an ordinary leather belt.

This Indian youngster, is playing clap sticks and is accompanied by a drummer.

'Hanske Knap'

The 'Hanske Knap' is a typical Flemish (Flanders is the Dutch-speaking area of Belgium) instrument and is made from an old wooden clog. On the evening of Twelfth Night, children go from house to house, singing and collecting money. They accompany their singing on a 'Hanske Knap' (Hans the Clapper). The money is put into Hanske's 'mouth'.
Originally the clogs were covered in rabbit's skin and cow's horns were fixed to them. This was to convince people that it would be better to satisfy Hanske by giving generously than to risk his anger by giving too little!

Making a Hanske Knap

All you need to make this traditional folk instrument is an wooden clog and a piece of thick cord.
Saw off the under part of the toe and then re-attach it with a leather or rubber hinge to form a flexible 'lower jaw'.
Bore a 4 mm hole in the 'chin', thread a length of cord through it and tie a knot in the end. Hanske's 'mouth' can now be made to 'clap' rhythmically by pulling the cord. The cord can also be decorated with beads or feathers.
Eyes and teeth (or any other decoration you wish) can now be painted on the Hanske Knap – an opportunity to use your imagination!

Below. The illustration shows how easy it is to make Hanske Knap. The hinge is made from a piece of rubber tire tube or thick leather.

Right. A Hanske Knap drawing by an unknown Flemish artist.

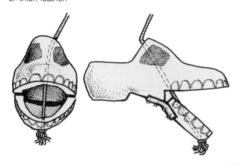

A traditional Hanske Knap chant

You never have a penny
or a nickel or a dime
to put in Hanske's mouth
It was six or seven years ago
when you gave the last time
poor Hans, poor Hans
please give Hans a dime
poor Hans ….

A Hanske Knap, an example of a typical Flemish folk instrument and made out of an old wooden clog.

Musical bottles

This is a very simple instrument to make and many variations are possible.

Not only bottles, but similar vessels such as pots, pans, cans or bowls can be used. The vessels are played by striking them with the hand or with a stick.

Differences in pitch are created by filling the vessels with varying quantities of water or sand. Variations in the size, thickness and material of the vessels also produce differences in pitch.

A variation of these musical bottles can be made from beakers or mugs, hung up by their handles and filled with different amounts of sand. Tins, pots and pans can also be used for making this instrument.

The simplest version of this instrument consists of a number of bottles which are completely or partly filled with water.

All you need to do to make this instrument is to put water in a few milk bottles or glasses and strike them with a small stick. Once you have worked out the right amounts of water and practiced for a while, you can soon play simple melodies.

Playing the musical bottles

The easiest way to make this instrument is to begin with a limited number of bottles, eight, for example. The left-hand bottle is almost filled with water. Play middle C on a piano or electric organ, strike the bottle and compare the pitch. Add or remove a little water until the bottle is 'tuned'. Repeat this operation for the other seven bottles, tuning them respectively to D, E, F, G, A, B and again C.

Tuning whistles or forks can also be used, of course.

You can now play your first tune. All you have to do is to remember the order of the notes and therefore you can quickly produce a pleasant melody!

The musical bottles produce a purer note when they are hanging rather than standing on a firm surface. A frame can be made from a steel tube or strong stick supported on two legs – or alternatively you can lay the support between two stools.

Fasten cords firmly around the necks of the bottles and tie them to the support. Try adding different amounts of water in order to produce different scales.

A variation of this instrument consists of cups or beakers hung up by their handles. A completely different sound than that made by the water-filled bottles can be produced by filling these beakers with different quantities of sand.

The playing sticks

The sticks can be made from two sturdy, straight pieces of elder wood. Remove the bark. Wrap a piece of cloth or felt around the thinner end and tie it securely with cotton thread. This will produce a fairly hard sound but a softer, warmer sound can be obtained by stuffing the cloth with cotton wadding. Of course, ordinary wooden spoons also make excellent playing sticks.

53

The straw xylophone

Originally the xylophone came from Indonesia and Africa but this model, the straw xylophone, comes from Flanders. The instrument consists of a series of tuned wooden bars arranged in order of pitch. This pitch order is known as a 'scale'.

A resonator is often placed under the bars to amplify the sound. There are many types of xylophone, including metallophones which have metal bars and marimbas which have carved wooden resonators. In this model, the straw xylophone, the resonator is formed from tightly-bound bundles of straw.

Making a straw xylophone

The soundbox
The soundbox of this instrument consists of bundles of straw bound together crosswise with thin strips of leather or velvet. The ends of the straw bundles are wrapped in cloth to help prevent damage.
The wooden staves which serve at the 'keys' are laid across the straw bundles.

The staves are held together with catgut or nylon thread and separated by thin wooden disks so that they can vibrate separately. The vibrations are amplified by the hollow stalks of straw, each straw acting as a small individual soundbox.

The staves

Quarter-sawn rosewood or pine is preferable for the staves. Quarter-sawn means that the wood is cut from the trunk at right angles to the heart of the tree. This gives the best-figured grain. By doing this the block of wood

has, in fact, been cut at 90° to the growth rings – hence the name: quarter-sawn (see page 11).

The width, length, thickness and the amount of material removed from the underside of the stave together determine its pitch. The longer and thicker the stave, the lower the pitch. In this model, the staves were made from 17×26 mm quarter-sawn pine.

To make this straw xylophone, you will need a total length of about 3 metres of timber. Use a plane to round off the top side slightly, then sandpaper thoroughly until the surface is very smooth.

Cut the staves to the lengths given in the table at bottom right. These are a little on the long side so that, if necessary, you can shorten them to obtain the right pitch before they are attached to the soundbox.

Tuning the staves

If you shave wood from under the ends of the

stave, the pitch becomes higher. On the other hand, if you make notches or sawcuts in the middle of the underside of the stave then the pitch becomes lower.

Tuning is carried out as follows: Begin on the left with the lowest pitch which can be tuned to the C of a piano or a tuning fork.

From left to right the pitch becomes increasingly higher: – D, E, F, G, A, B and C. Other scales can be obtained by moving the straw bundles inwards or outwards.

Bore holes through the ends of the staves and mount them, separated by disks, on a length of nylon thread (see illustration). Lay the mounted staves on the soundbox.

Playing the straw xylophone

Xylophones are preferably played with sticks, approximately 20 cm in length, cut from a single piece of wood. An example is shown in the illustration.

When learning to play melodies, it is best to begin with a simple tune which is easy to remember, such as a children's nursery rhyme. With a little practice you will soon be able to play a large number of melodies!

Stave lengths for the straw xylophone

Note: these lengths are a little on the long side so that, during assembly, the staves can be shortened to produce the right pitch.

do-295 mm	la -230 mm
re -290 mm	ti -220 mm
mi-275 mm	do-210 mm
fa -257 mm	re -200 mm
sol-240 mm	mi-190 mm
	fa -180 mm
	sol-170 mm

The stick is cut from a piece of hardwood. This illustration shows one of the many possible shapes.

The staves are made from quarter-sawn pine wood (see p. 11).

A straw xylophone during construction. This instrument consists of pine staves set on a soundbox of bundles of straw.

Clap sticks

Clap sticks in the shape of small hands were known in ancient Egypt and were probably used instead of actually clapping the hands themselves. Clap sticks in one form or another have been known in practically every culture.

Clap sticks consist of two almost identical sticks which are struck one against the other. Usually the hand is used to strike the two clap sticks together (see photo) but it is also possible to hang up small pieces of wood (or some other material) close together so that the wind blows them against each other.

Making traditional clap sticks

Clap sticks, or clappers, come in all shapes and sizes. The simplest form consists of two identical pieces of wood or bone. Every material has its own 'colour' of tone. Highly suitable types of hardwood for making clap sticks are walnut, rosewood and plum. Saw two identical pieces, measuring approximately 4×15 cm, from a piece of wood 7 mm in thickness. One end of each piece is now tapered. This can be done with a saw or a plane. Sandpaper the surface smooth and harden this end in an open fire. This makes the clap sticks sound much louder. Remove the black sooty deposits with sandpaper. Decorate the sticks to your own taste.

Playing the clapsticks
One clap stick is held firmly between the middle finger and ring finger. This stick is the one which 'claps' the other. The second clap stick is held tightly between the thumb and the forefinger. This stick does not move. The two tapered ends of the clap sticks clap against each other. The sound is produced by a rythmical movement of the hand and wrist. The hollow of your hands forms the soundbox. If the moving clap stick tends to slide out of your fingers, bore a hole about 2 cm from the end. If you place the knuckle of your middle finger in this hole, it will support the stick and prevent it sliding out of your hand.

Everybody is familiar with clap sticks (or clappers). But not everybody can play them... Here you can see various types of clap sticks made from wood and bone.

A children's clap stick song
Clapper-de-clapper-de-clap-clap-clap
Clapper-de-clapper-de-clap-clap-clap
Clap sticks claps sticks one two three
Clap sticks are the thing for me
Clapper-de-clapper-de-clap-clap-clap

Clapper-de-clapper-de-clap-clap-clap
Clapper-de-clapper-de-clap-clap-clap
Clap sticks claps sticks one two three
Clap sticks are the thing for me
Clapper-de-clapper-de-clap-clap-clap

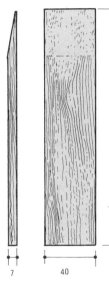

This illustration shows the dimensions of the clap sticks. After the ends have been diagonally cut, they are hardened over an open flame.

150

7   40

Jester's clapper made from a single piece of wood. The strips (or 'lamina') are cut with the aid of a circular saw or a jigsaw. The handle can be made in any shape or form you fancy.

The illustration shows the dimensions and shape of the jester's clapper. The thinner the lamina, the better the sound produced.

The jester's clapper

A jester's clapper is best made out of hardwood which does not splinter. Walnut, rosewood and plum are all suitable for making this variation of the clap sticks.

Making the jester's clapper
The block of wood should measure approximately 35×5×3.5 cm, but fairly wide variations in size are possible. The basic rule is that the shorter the tongues, the thinner they must be in order to 'clap' in a satisfactory manner.
Using a try square, draw a line around the wood 10 cm from one end. This end will be the handle. Mark lines for the sawcuts for the tongues, each tongue is 5mm thick and runs through to the end of the handle.
The easiest way to cut the tongues is with a jigsaw or a circular saw (equipped with a guide) but a hand saw can be used if you do not have access to such equipment.
Now smooth thoroughly the inside surfaces, the sides and edges of the tongues using a piece of folded sandpaper. Now shape the handle using a rasp and file. Sandpaper it smooth. The handle can be any shape you wish and decorated to your own taste – but remember that it must lie naturally and comfortably in the hand. Finally rub the handle well with linseed oil or varnish it – this helps prevent it becoming dirty.

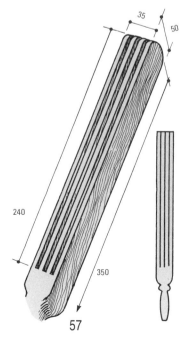

35

50

240

350

57

An illustration of a
tongue (or 'hinged')
clapper and a 'bird
scarer'. Both these
instruments are easier to
play than the free-
standing clap sticks.

The tongue clapper

This instrument consists of three similar clappers. Two of these form the body and the third is hinged between them.

Making the tongue clapper

The tongue clapper is made from a piece of 9 mm rosewood (or similar hardwood). The dimensions of the clapper can vary somewhat but the two outer tongues should be approximately 4×15 cm and the inner piece some 8 cm longer so that the handle fits nicely into the hand. Note: You may find it easier to cut the inner tongue and handle in two separate pieces.

Use the grid to enlarge the patterns to the desired size and transfer them to the wood. Cut the two outer tongues, the inner tongue and the handle using a fretsaw or electric bandsaw. Cut the two trapezium-shaped side pieces from plywood. Sandpaper each piece thoroughly, rounding the edges slightly. Bore holes through the 'ears' of the inner tongue and the 'tongue' of the handle – as indicated in the illustration – and hinge the two pieces together with a nail or a screw. The inner tongue, of course, should move freely from side to side.

The instrument can now be assembled. Glue the two side pieces to the outer tongues and the handle (see the photograph left). The tongues can now be hardened by holding them in an open flame. Sandpaper any sooty deposit away and decorate the instrument to your own taste.

The end of the handle can be furnished with a drawer knob – these can be bought, ready-made, in all shapes and sizes and in a wide variety of materials.

Playing the tongue clapper

Playing this instrument might appear simple at first sight – but listen sometime to a Spanish dancer playing the castanets! The most difficult trick to master is the rhythmical movement the hand must make in order to produce a continuous, unbroken sound. The movement actually originates in the wrist – which moves rapidly back and forth – in combination with the fingers.

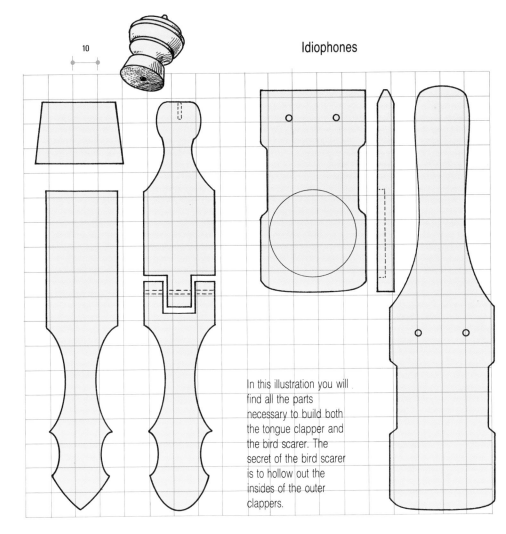

In this illustration you will find all the parts necessary to build both the tongue clapper and the bird scarer. The secret of the bird scarer is to hollow out the insides of the outer clappers.

Practice this movement while listening to a record of Spanish music.

Once you can follow the rhythm of the castanets, you have little more to learn!

The musical possibilities of the instrument can be increased by using the clapper as a stick to play, for example, a side drum or a tambourine.

The bird scarer

Making a bird scarer

In Russia, this instrument is used rather like castanets with a handle. It consists of three wooden tongues bound together with a length of cord.

Use a piece of hardwood about 5 mm thick. Again, the precise dimensions of the handle and tongues can vary to some extent, but the handle should be approximately 17×4 cm and the tongues approximately 8×4 cm. Use the grid to enlarge the shapes to the required size, transfer them to the wood and cut them out with a fretsaw or bandsaw. Clamp the three pieces together and bore two holes in the positions indicated in the illustration. The pieces can be hardened over an open flame and any sooty deposit sandpapered off.

The inner sides of two outer tongues are now hollowed out using a gouge or scraper and then sandpapered smooth. These hollows form the soundbox and increase the loudness of the bird scarer considerably!

The three pieces are now attached together with a stout cord – and you are ready to go out and begin scaring those birds!

You can play a tune immediately with two everyday tablespoons.

The musical saw and the singing glass

Both the musical saw and the singing glass belong to the family of friction idiophones. Other 'ready-made' instruments, such as sea shells and pine cones also belong to this group. The sound is produced with the aid of a wet finger, a cloth, string, stick or even a bow.
In the eighteenth and nineteenth centuries in particular, the so-called 'glass harmonica' was popular. Complete compositions were played on glasses of various size and thickness. The glasses were revolved mechanically through a bowl of water so that the rims always remained wet.

One does not come across the musical saw very often these days, but in the United States it is still a popular instrument with blue-grass bands, groups which specialize in a particular form of country music.

The musical saw – in Europe usually played by clowns – is a favorite instrument with blue grass bands

in the United States. Piet Hohmann (who drew the illustrations for this book) shows how the saw is played.

The song of the saw

Every saw can 'sing', but the best effect is achieved with a long, flexible saw. The best length is about 60 to 70 cm.
Hold the handle of the saw firmly between your knees or feet, the teeth pointing towards you. Make sure that the teeth do not come in contact with your clothing – not only might this damage your clothes, but it also spoils the sound!
The saw can be played by striking it with a stick or by stroking it with a bow – a bow can be bought for a few dollars in a music store but you can easily make one yourself (see page 89).

Take the end of the blade between the thumb and fingers of one hand and hold the bow in the other – if you are right-handed, hold the bow in the right hand; if you are left-handed, hold it in your left. Various notes can be extracted from the saw by bending the blade by pressing downwards against it with your thumb. This creates a tension in the saw and this tension must always be maintained – except for a few very high notes.

In order to find the correct notes, tap the saw with a stick while steadily increasing the downward pressure of your thumb. With the aid of a piano or a tuning fork, find the exact place on the saw that gives an A. This will lie approximately in the middle of the blade. Mark this position with chalk (mark it later with a spot of paint) so that you can find it again. The next note is B which lies nearer the upper edge of the saw. F is both the highest and lowest note.

Another important element in playing the saw is the vibration. This is achieved by making a rapid movement with the hand holding the saw or with the aid of the leg which is pressed against the handle. This vibration is necessary to create a round, rich sound from the saw.

The song of the glass

Any stemmed glass can be made to 'sing' and the only 'equipment' you need to produce this song is a wet finger! Hold the glass firmly by the foot of the stem and rub your wetted finger around the rim. The glass will soon produce a plaintive note. The faster you rub and the greater pressure you exert on the foot of the glass, the more powerful the 'song'. Note: When a glass vibrates at its resonant frequency, it might shatter – therefore you must take care!

The singing glass as a musical instrument. A plaintive tone can be created by rubbing the rim of the glass with your wetted finger.

The notched stick

In previous centuries, a notched stick was used to keep note of credit. Each time a glass of beer or a loaf of bread was bought 'on credit' a new notch was cut into the stick. When the stick was full then the account had to be paid and no excuses! In common parlance someone who had 'to many notches on his stick' was not to be entirely trusted!

The illustration shows how simple it is to make a notched stick.

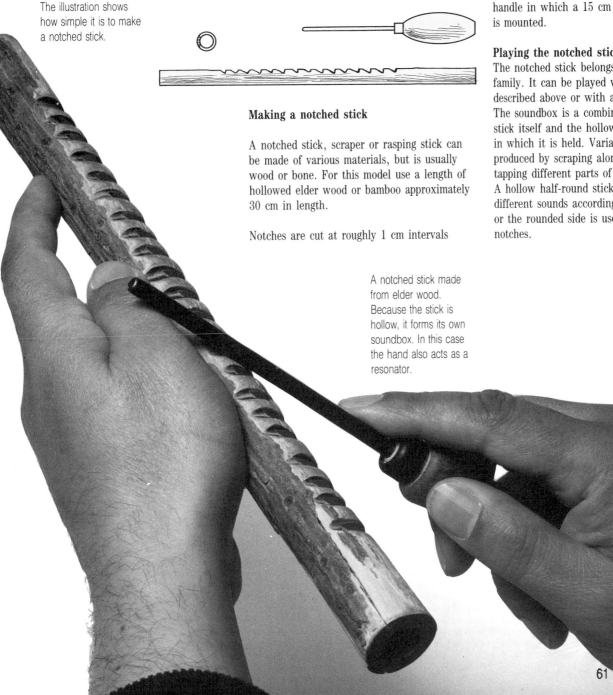

A notched stick made from elder wood. Because the stick is hollow, it forms its own soundbox. In this case the hand also acts as a resonator.

Making a notched stick

A notched stick, scraper or rasping stick can be made of various materials, but is usually wood or bone. For this model use a length of hollowed elder wood or bamboo approximately 30 cm in length.

Notches are cut at roughly 1 cm intervals along one side using a sharp hobby knife or a triangular file. Leave about 5 cm at each end free of notches. The notches should be cut just deep enough to make small holes as they break through to the hollow interior. The inner wall of the stick must be smooth and clean so that the sound is as pure as possible. A playing stick is also needed. This is made from a file handle in which a 15 cm length of 6 mm steel is mounted.

Playing the notched stick

The notched stick belongs to scraped idiophone family. It can be played with the stick described above or with an ordinary pencil. The soundbox is a combination of the hollow stick itself and the hollow shape of the hand in which it is held. Variations in sound can be produced by scraping along the notches, tapping different parts of the stick, and so on. A hollow half-round stick produces still different sounds according to whether the edge or the rounded side is used to scrape the notches.

The hunchback rattle

The hunchback rattle was typically an instrument for Shrove Tuesday or Mardi Gras singers. They went from house to house, collecting money and singing the traditional song: 'Hunchback rattle, violin and bass, put some money in the tin and we will play for you'.

The traditional hunchback rattle

Like the Hanske Knap, hunchback rattles are found in a wide variety of shapes and sizes – the one described here is the traditional form. But, of course, you are perfectly free to give this instrument your own more modern interpretation!

For the body of the hunchback, you require a sheet of plywood measuring approximately 20×40 cm and 12 mm in thickness. Use the grid to enlarge the shape in the correct proportions to the largest size possible. Cut out the shape with a fretsaw or bandsaw and sandpaper it thoroughly. The hole in the center is sawn out with a fretsaw blade (drill a large hole in one corner so that you can insert the blade). The 'ribs' of the hunchback will be mounted in this hole.

The ribs

The ribs of the hunchback consists of four metal plates with three wooden plates of the same size and shape inserted between them. The wooden plates are cut out of a piece of hardwood, hardened over an open flame and sandpapered clean and smooth. Holes, 3 mm in diameter, are bored through the centerline of the plates 1 cm from the top and bottom shorter edges.

The body of the hunchback is now mounted in a drill stand and two 3 mm holes drilled from the back of the body towards the front at a slightly downwards angle. These holes are the same distance apart as those in the plates (see illustration).

The ribs are now mounted in the rib cage on long nails glued into the plywood body. Give the hunchback a final rub down with sandpaper and decorate it either in the traditional colors shown in the illustration – or in colors in your own choice.

Four metal plates with three sheets of wood between them together form the ribs of this instrument.

The grid in the illustration is a useful aid in enlarging the hunchback rattle to the required size. It can then be painted in the same colors as the model on page 63.

Making the rasping stick

Use the grid in the illustration to enlarge the pattern to the required size, transfer it to a piece of plywood, saw out the shape and sandpaper it thoroughly. The stick can then be painted in the same colors as the hunchback itself.

Playing the hunchback rattle

This instrument is also a scraped idiophone. Hold the hunchback firmly by its feet and play it by drawing the rasping stick across the ribs. The sound is varied by varying the tempo of the rasping stick. A notched stick (see page 61) can also be used as a rasping stick.

A colorful model of a hunchback rattle. This is the traditional Flemish model but, of course, that should not stop you making a version of your own.

63

The cog rattle

Cog rattles make a loud, penetrating noise. Traditionally they were used by night watchmen and lepers. Night watchmen used them to wake up the sleeping population in the early morning. Lepers used them to warn healthy people of their approach.

Cog rattles belong to the family of scraped instruments in which sound is produced by drawing a thin strip of wood over a series of notches. In the cog rattle, a strip of wood flicks over a notched wheel when the rattle is rotated. There are countless versions of this type of rattle, a few of which are illustrated on these pages.

Making a cog rattle

Cog rattles are found in a wide variety of shapes and sizes, but they all work on the same principle – scraping a tongue over a cog wheel. The rattle described here is simple but very effective and is made with bits and pieces of scrap materials.

Take a cardboard tube or a large bamboo of a diameter of about 5 cm and cut off a piece of 4 cm in depth. Glue wrapping paper over one end and decorate the sides with paint or colored paper. The soundbox is now ready!

Take a piece of soft wood or bamboo about 30 cm long and 1 cm thick. Mark the middle point and then on both sides of this, half the diameter of the soundbox ± 2.5 cm. At these two points carefully cut halfway through the wood. Bend it into a U-shape, and fix the soundbox between the ends with small nails or screws. Brush wood glue into the bends in order to strengthen them.

Now carefully bore a hole, 7 mm in diameter, in each leg approximately 7 cm from the soundbox.

The cog wheel

Take a length of soft wood measuring about 20 cm × 9 mm. Using a sharp hobby knife, whittle down the last 7 cm of one end of the wood so that it is thin enough to pass through the holes in the legs. When mounted it should therefore protrude about 2 cm. Another way to make the handle is to use a thin stick and thicken the last 13 cm or so with adhesive tape or strips of cloth. The handle of a file or screwdriver also makes an excellent handle. Bore it out so that it fits over the end of the stick and glue it firmly in position.

Use a sharp knife to split that part of the wood which lies between the two legs. Cut two 1 × 2 cm rectangles out of a tin can, push them through the split and bend them to form the four 'teeth' of the cog wheel (see the illustration).

Several cog rattles of various shapes and sizes, including both traditional and modern examples.

64

An Indonesian rattle with
a soundbox in the form
of a small drum.

125

50

75

40

15

7

20

10

50

70

200

9

The illustration shows all
the parts needed to build
an Indonesian cog rattle,
together with their
dimensions.

All dimensions are in millimetres

The tongue

The tongue consists of a length of bamboo
which fits exactly between the cog wheel and
the middle of the soundbox. Stretch a strong
rubber band over the legs of the rattle, insert
the tongue and twist it tightly. This is done by
moving the tongue up and down between the
band and turning it in a counter-clockwise
direction. The rattle is now ready to play.
Note: Always keep a few strong rubber bands
in reserve!

65

The Jew's harp

The Jew's harp, or mouth harp, is an extremely old idiophone yet it is one of the least known. For centuries it was played by young men in love; the seductive, soft sound intended to convince the lady in question that she was the only one for him.

The instrument consists of a flexible tongue mounted in a metal or wooden frame. This frame fits exactly into the open mouth. You can purchase metal Jew's harps for a few dollars but you can make wooden or bamboo versions quite easily yourself.

'Boy with Jew's harp', by Dirck van Baburen. (Centraal Museum Utrecht).

Three examples of the Jew's harp. The models above and left are modern variations. The model on the right is made of wrought iron and dates from the nineteenth century.

Making a Jew's harp

In a heteroglottal Jew's harp, the tongue is not cut from the frame but is attached separately. The heteroglottal instrument described here consists of a flexible bamboo tongue mounted in a plywood frame.

To make the body of the Jew's harp you need a piece of 4 mm plywood measuring approximately 3 × 7 cm. Enlarge, transfer and cut out the shape using a fretsaw. Bore holes for the fastenings and glue the bridge in position (see illustration).

A length of split bamboo, about 12 cm long, is used as the tongue. Bind this in place with strong thread or thin wire.

Sandpaper both the frame and the tongue.

Playing the Jew's harp

The Jew's harp is played by holding the frame against the open lips. Breathe in and out steadily and at the same time pluck the tongue with one finger. Your mouth forms the soundbox of this instrument. The pitch and tone color produced depend on the positions of the lips, cheeks and teeth. The sound is also heavily influenced by the way in which you breathe in and out while you are playing.

10

The illustration shows how to make a Jew's harp from a piece of plywood and a tapered bamboo stick.

A scale which – with practise – you can play on a Jew's harp.

The sansa

The sansa or 'thumb piano', like the Jew's harp, is an idiophone in which the sound is produced by plucking flexible tongues. The sansa is a typically African instrument. The resonator can be a simple plank of wood or a hollow box. There are also sansas built into a hollow shape, such as a gourd, which then forms the resonator. This sound can be imitated by placing (and playing) the instrument in, for example, an empty bucket.

This is an original sansa from Central Africa. The sansa, or 'thumb piano', is a typical African instrument.

Making a sansa

An ordinary large cigar box is used for the soundbox of the sansa. A sound hole is cut to the left of the center of the lid. This can be any shape you like. First bore a large hole and then complete the hole using first a keyhole saw and then a fretsaw.

A flat strip of wood, approximately 2 mm thick and 1 cm wide is glued across the top right-hand edge of the lid. At a distance of 10 cm from this strip, a second strip — triangular of half-round in cross-section — approximately 1 cm thick is glued across the lid (see illustration).

The sansa described on these pages is built from a cigar box and ten hacksaws. The illustration shows how the parts fit together to form the finished instrument.

The tongues

Now take ten fretsaw or hacksaw blades, about 20 cm in length, and remove the pins from the ends. Lay the blades in two groups of five across the two strips of wood. Now place a strip of narrow half-round molding across the blades about halfway between the two original strips. Mark the positions — on both sides of each blade — at which holes must be bored in the lid. Bore the holes using a 1 mm drill. Now thread nylon thread or thin wire through these holes to attach the cross piece and so hold the blades in position. The thread should be drawn tight enough to hold the blades firmly in position, but not so tight that the blades touch the lid of the box.

Now glue the lid on the box and decorate to your own taste — patterns can be carved with a hobby knife, burned in with a hot awl or simply painted in bright colors. The box can be held over a heat source to harden it. This improves the sound quality.

Playing the sansa

This instrument is tuned by moving the blades backwards and forwards under the cross piece. The further back the blade, the higher the pitch. Begin with the first group of five blades. Play A on a piano and move the blade on the far left backwards and forwards until it sounds as close as possible to the A. Now tune the next blade to B and so on. The second group of blades is tuned in a similar manner. The blade on the far right is tuned to F, the next to G and so on. Try to work with tones and not with semitones. The sansa is certainly not the easiest instrument to tune and you may find that it needs frequent retuning — but the mellow sound it produces makes all the extra effort well worth while.

Once the instrument has been tuned to your satisfaction, lay it on your lap with the playing ends of the blades towards you. Pluck the blades with your thumbs — more complex melodies may also require the use of your fingers.

Membranophones

Membranophones are instruments in which the sound is produced by a membrane — a tensioned sheet or skin. There are two members of the family, drums and mirlitons, drums being by far the more important. The sound is created by making the membrane vibrate by striking it or brushing it with sticks or the hands. In the lesser-known mirliton the sound is created by humming into it.

Drums are among the oldest instruments in the history of mankind. Excavations and drawings have proved that drums existed some 4000 years ago in Mesopotamia and Egypt. Many cultures also accorded magical powers to this instrument. The magicians of the Laplanders used a magic drum to make known the will of the gods. The great Portuguese drums — the bombos — are well-known. Around the thirteenth century in England and France drums were played by itinerant musicians, often together with the flute. The side drum was traditionally played on the field of battle — not only to overawe the enemy but also to signal one's own troops. Today, drums are used in every form of music — by folk music ensembles, dance bands, pop groups and symphony orchestras.

A young Indian monk from the monastery in Sikkim plays a drum during a religious séance. This drum is very similar to the side drum we know in the West.

This engraving shows two revelers on their way to a celebration. As they dance along they are accompanying themselves on flute and tambourine.

How membranophones work

Sound is vibrations. The stretched skin of a membranophone can be made to vibrate in different ways – by striking it or rubbing it, for example. The vibration in the skin is passed into the body of the instrument which acts as an amplifier. A membranophone is usually struck with sticks or brushes. Of course, the hand can also be used – as with many South American dance orchestras. Rattle drums, in which sound is produced by small beads and friction drums, in which a stick is pushed through the skin and moved from side to side, are also found.
The shape and size of the instrument body determines the volume of sound it produces.

Various body shapes
Membranophones are found in many different shapes and sizes and they are usually classified according to the body shape.
Cylindrical drums (A) are straight-sided, for example while conical drums (B) slope from top to bottom. Barrel drums (C) – as the name suggests – are barrel-shaped and thus have bulging sides.
Long drums (G) are made in a variety of shapes but the length determines the pitch.
In frame drums (H), the body is almost non-existent and the skin is stretched over a light frame. Kettledrums (I) have a vessel or pot body and a single playing head.
There are drums in the shape of an hour-glass (D) and a goblet (E). Finally there are the footed drums (F) which have legs that are cut from the body of the drum.

Vibrating membranes
In a membranophone sound is produced by striking a stretched membrane so causing it to vibrate (A). These vibrations are amplified by the body of the drum and so become audible to the human ear. A mirliton is sounded by blowing or humming into the instrument (B).

Skin attachment
Animal skin can be used for the drum skin – goat or calf skin is preferable because it is thin and supple. The disadvantage is that these skins are fairly expensive. A good alternative is a cow's bladder which can be obtained for almost nothing from an abattoire – (some abattoires sell prepared bladders for making drum skins). The skin can be attached to the body in four ways: it may be glued (A), nailed (B), pegged (C) or laced (D).

Lacing the skin
Different styles of lacing are employed for attaching drum skins. Some of these styles are illustrated here. From left to right: these patterns show N-lacing (A), W-lacing (B), X-lacing (C), Y-lacing (D) and lastly net-lacing (E). Other forms of lacing are occasionally found but these five are the most commonly used.

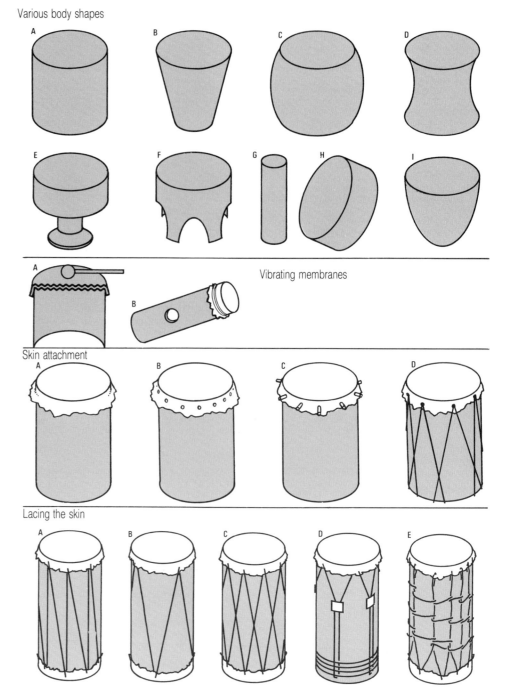

Various body shapes

Vibrating membranes

Skin attachment

Lacing the skin

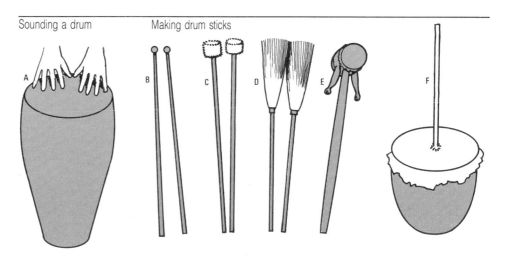

Tuning

A drum is tuned by altering the tension of the drum skin (also known as the playing head). This can be carried out in different ways: by adjusting the lacing (A), by positioning and moving small blocks under the lacing (B) or by turning tuning keys or taps (C). Tone quality can be changed by applying small sticky balls or paste to the playing head.

Playing heads

A drum may be single-headed with only one skin (A) or double-headed with a skin at each end (B). Double-headed drums may be played on one head only or on both heads.

Sounding a drum

There are various methods of making a drum skin vibrate. It can be beaten with the hands (A), with sticks (B), with padded sticks (C) or with brushes – usually made of wire, but can also be stiff hair or even thinly sliced bamboo (D). The skin of the clapper drum (E) is struck with small beads, attached by cords, as the drum is shaken. Most friction drums (F) are played by means of a stick that pierces the skin and is attached to its underside.

Making drum sticks

You can make sticks quite easily yourself from lengths of oak or some similar hardwood. Saw off a straight length, about 35 cm in length and 2 cm in diameter, using an ordinary tenon saw. This should now be made round and smooth. Use a plane or – better still – a lathe – to do this.

Make a groove at a distance of 2 cm from the narrower end of the stick and, using a sharp knife, carve the last 2 cm into the shape of a rounded candle flame.

Sandpaper this head and then varnish the stick. Another method is to glue a cork or wooden ball to the end of the stick.

In order to ensure the strongest possible bond between ball and stick, use a 4 cm × 4 mm nail. Using a 4 mm drill, bore 2.5 cm deep holes in the end of the stick and in the ball. Glue the nail into the stick, ensuring that at least 1.5 cm is protruding, and nip off the head with a pair of pincers. Now glue the ball to the outstanding nail.

The sound produced when the stick strikes the drum stick can be 'dampened' by wrapping

Tuning

Playing heads

Sounding a drum   Making drum sticks

cloth or felt around the head of the stick. Brushes can be made from lengths of bamboo. Choose two pieces approximately 30 cm long and 12 mm in diameter. It is important to choose pieces which have nodes about 10 cm from the narrower end. Cut a groove under this node using a hacksaw.

To make the 'brush': cut long, thin strips from this groove to the end of the stick, using a fine, sharp knife. Now sand the whole stick – including the brush strips – with fine sandpaper and varnish.

Hair and wire brushes can be bought quite cheaply in any music store.

The cylindrical drum

Cylindrical and conical drums are the commonest types of tubular drum.

They are known in various cultures throughout the world and are used both by tribes in Central Africa and North American Indians. Cylindrical drums vary considerably in size, but they are true cylinders in that the internal diameter of a particular drum is exactly the same at any point along its length. They may be single or double headed (have a skin at one end or both).

Making a cylindrical drum

To make this instrument you need a cylindrical body and one or two drum skins. The dimensions of the body will depend on what material is available to you but as a rule of thumb you may assume that the bigger the body, the deeper and heavier the sound it will produce. You also require two pieces of cord – one fairly thick and the other somewhat thinner – of a length equal to at least four times the circumference of the body of the

An example of a cylindrical drum. This model was built without a tension frame and is double-headed (it has skins at both ends).

74

drum. You also need a few bits of leather or copper wire.

Begin by making the drum body. Large, round soap powder cartons are very suitable but you can also buy a length of plastic tubing from a builder's merchant or a do-it-yourself store. This tubing is available in many different diameters.

Before you mount the drum skins, make sure that the body contains no sharp edges. Round the edges off with a rasp or file and sandpaper them smooth. Now bore seven holes at a distance of approximately 1 cm from the lower rim of the drum body. These holes have a diameter of 6 mm and the distances between them should be as equal as possible

(illustration 1, page 76).

Now wet the skin and lay it over the open end of the body. Fold the edges down over the sides and press them firmly against the body (2). When the skin is almost dry, cut U-shaped indentations above each of the seven holes in the body of the drum. Fasten a length of thick cord tightly round the drum body (3). Brush wood glue on the protruding part of the flaps and fold these back over the cord (4).

Now wrap a length of thinner cord over the folded flaps above the thicker cord. This should encircle the body three times (5). Fold the flaps back over this cord ring and again brush wood glue onto the outside of the flaps (6). A second ring of thin cord, again brushed

Two young street musicians in Morocco, one with a drum, the other with rattles.

An effective drum can be made from simple materials – an empty soap-powder container, a drumskin, a macramé ring and cord.

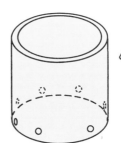

Membranophones

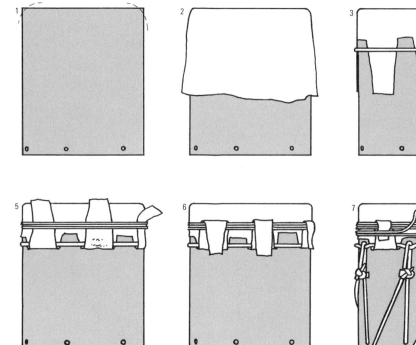

The illustrations above show how a drum is assembled. The skin is stretched by means of cords around which leather laces are knotted. This knot is clearly illustrated.

All dimensions are in millimetres

150

with glue, is now fastened tightly over the ends of the flaps (7).

The drum skins can now be tensioned in the following manner: A thin cord – the 'tensioning cord' – is passed over the thicker cord between two flaps and through the 6 mm hole directly below. It is then led up and over the cord between the next two flaps and back through the hole below that. This process is repeated around the drum. This method of attaching the skin is known as the 'N-form' (see page 72) but you can use any of the other methods shown. A wood or metal ring, which fits exactly over the body of the drum, can be used instead of cord. The flaps are folded and glued over this and the tensioning cord fitted in the way described above. When the glue has dried, the cord is tightened and knotted behind the last hole. Extra tension can be obtained by fitting copper wire rings to the tensioning cord. Extra tension is obtained by pushing these downwards. The same effect is

obtained with strips of leather. These should be knotted as shown in the illustration above right.

Playing the cylindrical drum
The cylindrical drum is a rhythm instrument and as such is particularly suitable as a background instrument in orchestras and bands. The drum is also valuable as a solo instrument. There is a multitude of ways in which drums can be played – a few of these are given here.

To begin with the drum can be played with the hands. This calls for a great deal of practise and it might be useful to listen to South American bands. Many rock'n roll bands also use bongos played in this way. If you are playing with drum sticks, the essential thing is to lift the sticks from the skin immediately after striking so that the sound is not adversely affected. Surprising sound effects can be obtained by playing various percussion

instruments together. The exact place where the skin is struck is important for the sound. High, clear tones are produced when the edge of the skin is struck; duller, heavier sounds are produced when the skin is struck in the center. The skin can also be dampened with the thumb or heel of the hand and this also creates differences in the pitch and tone color of the sound.

The pan drum

This is a very versatile drum. It consists of a number of drums of different heights but of the same diameter. Because each drum has a different height, each has a different pitch, and it is therefore possible to produce a wide range of sounds from this instrument. With a little matching and measuring you can make a combination from which you can extract a terrific sound.

Pan drums are known in Africa, of course, but are also commonly used in Europe and North America.

The simplest way to build a pan drum is with a number of cardboard cylinders and transparent paper. After the paper has been glued over the heads of the cylinders it is treated with a coat of lacquer. This tensions the paper.

The drum skins do not need to be of leather or a pig's bladder; stiff transparent paper, treated with model airplane lacquer, does the job very well indeed. Glue this paper over the end of the tube and lacquer it as soon as the glue is dry. As already mentioned, the pitch depends on the body of the drum – a long drum gives a low pitch, a short drum a high pitch. The tension of the skin also influences the pitch. Cut the cardboard tubes to the required length using a hacksaw.

Making a pan drum

The principle of the pan drum is the same as that of the cylindrical drum. A series of cylindrical drums can therefore be made in the same way, each drum in the series being of a different height and therefore having a different pitch. There is, however, a much simpler way of making the pan drum. You need several cardboard tubes of different lengths but of the same diameter. You can make as many drums as you like – the more you have, the more unlimited the musical possibilities.

Playing the pan drum

The pan drum is played in much the same way as the cylindrical drum – with the fingers, sticks, brushes, and so on. Much practise is required in order to be able to exploit the possibilities of this instrument to the full, but the end result is impressive! The pan drum is particularly suitable for use as a solo instrument.

The frame drum

The frame drum is a drum which consists of one or two membranes stretched over a simple frame. This frame is made of thin wood. Usually the frame drum is rather shallow. Earlier, these frames were made from metal rings obtained from barrels of chewing tobacco, but nowadays other materials are used because this type of barrel is no longer obtainable.

Making a frame drum

Birch plywood, 7 mm in thickness, is used to make the frame of this instrument. Other suitable woods are beech, maple, elm and walnut. The basic requirement is that the wood should be flexible and bend easily. Again, the playing head can consist of different materials, such as well-cleaned pig's bladder or thick paper treated with model

This version of the double-skinned drum is made from a barrel hoop over which two drum skins are lashed.

Right: A young man from Tanzania playing his own version of the double-skinned drum.

Membranophones

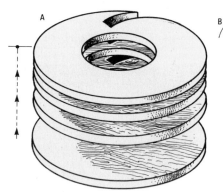

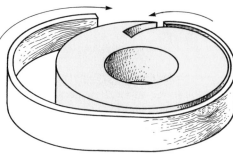

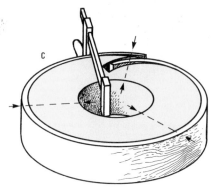

A mold is necessary for making the frame of both a drum and a tambourine. This mold is made from layers of fibreboard. This is an excellent aid when you have to bend wood. The arrows in illustration C indicate the points where the clamps must be positioned.

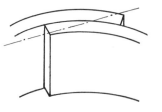

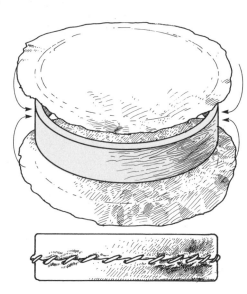

airplane lacquer. This is available in hobby stores and do-it-yourself stores.

Making the frame

A mold, or template, is required to form the frame. The diameter of this mold is the same as the internal diameter of the frame. The finished frame will be 60 to 70 mm in width. The mold is built up from disks of the required diameter cut from fibreboard. You will need three or four of these, depending on the thickness of the board. Glue the disks together and cut out a slot slightly wider than the birch plywood (see illustration). Cut a hole through the center of the mold to contain the clamps. The plywood strip from which the frame is made should be approximately 150 mm longer than the circumference of the finished frame, because the ends must overlap before they can be glued together. Set the plywood in boiling water for half-an-hour and then bend it around the mold using a series of clamps. Allow the ends to overlap (see illustration C above) so that they can be later cut and glued. Leave the frame in the clamps for a week or so until the wood has dried out thoroughly. When the plywood is dry, it is ready to be glued. The ends are overlapped and cut diagonally with a tenon saw (see illustration). Brush glue onto the two cut surfaces and – with the aid of the mold – clamp these surfaces together (see illustration E). Set the frame aside and allow the glue to dry for at least two or three hours. The frame should now be sandpapered thoroughly. This applies particularly to the edges – otherwise

the skin may be damaged.

The frame drum is a double-headed drum. A wet skin is stretched over each end of the frame and the two stitched together with strong cord or a leather strip. It is important that the two heads are tensioned properly, otherwise the instrument will be unplayable. The photograph on page 78 and the illustration at the foot of the center column indicate how the skins should be stitched together. Ensure that the cord is not too close to the edge of the skin as it might then tear it.

The sticks

The sticks can be made from bamboo. Wrap thin strips of cloth around the end and fasten them in place with thin string. The stick in the photograph on page 78 is furnished with a machine-made soft head. A large bead or a piece of cork can also be used. These are wrapped in cloth and glued to the end of the stick. They are again wrapped in cloth and fastened in place with thin string.

Playing the frame drum

The frame drum is also a rhythm instrument and is therefore ideal as support for an orchestra. Various percussion instruments can be used in conjunction with it. As with all percussion instruments, it is important to lift the stick immediately the skin is struck, otherwise the sound is deadened.

The tambourine

Many people associate the tambourine with Spanish flamenco dancers or marching bands, but it has a much greater potential. The tambourine is quite easy to make and to play and it forms a good basis for the rhythm section of any musical group. It also gives the player an opportunity to display a degree of virtuosity – an unexpected syncopated accompaniment, perhaps, or a spectacularly athletic display in which the tambourine is hurled high into the air and (hopefully!) caught as it comes down.

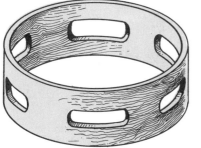

The disks are made to the instructions given under rattles (p. 47), and mounted as shown in the illustration. The heads of the nails are either cut off or recessed in the frame.
The skin is fixed in position with staples or round-headed pins.

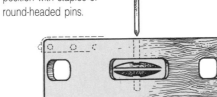

It is well worth the trouble of making your own tambourine instead of buying one, because you can make it to the exact size you want.

Making a tambourine

Like the instrument just described, the tambourine is a frame drum and therefore the first thing to do is to make a frame! The instructions for this can be found on the opposite page.

When the frame is ready a series of oval holes must be cut into the side. Set a marking gauge to one-third the width of the frame and mark two lines (one from the top and one from bottom) around the outer side. Measure the circumference using a flexible tape measure and divide this by six. This is the distance between the centers of the oval holes. At these distances mark six lines at right angles to the lines already drawn. Now mark further lines 3 cm either side of these lines. You have now marked six rectangles spaced at equal distances on the outer frame. Bore 'starter' holes in each rectangle and cut them out using a fretsaw. Round off the inside edges with a rasp and sandpaper.

Exactly in the center of each hole (you have the marked line to guide you) drill a hole vertically downwards (see illustration at the foot of the middle column). Make the bells or metal disks according to the instructions given for the rattle on page 47. These are fixed in the oval holes by means of a nail or a piece thick steel wire. The tops of these nails should be recessed into the rim and the heads covered with a blob of wax.

The whole frame is now sandpapered again. The wetted skin (again, different materials can be used) is stretched over the frame and stapled in position – (a more pleasant effect is obtained by using decorative round-headed panel pins to fix the playing head in position).

Playing the tambourine
The tambourine is played with the knuckles, the palm of the hand or the fingers – or a combination of all three! With a little practise, you will be able to obtain very rhythmical results on this instrument.

The rommelpot

The rommelpot belongs to that distinctive family of drums known as friction drums. The membrane is not vibrated by striking it, but rather by means of friction — being rubbed with the fingers or a cloth, or by a stick or cord piercing the membrane. The instrument consists of a container — a flowerpot, a large can or something similar — over which is stretched a membrane. The rommelpot was used mostly during folk festivals, such as Twelfth Night (Epiphany), when traveling musicians went from door to door, singing for money and food.

·₃ KONINGHEN·

Making a rommelpot

Making a rommelpot is really quite easy. A pig's or cow's bladder can usually be obtained from an abattoire — otherwise you can use one of the alternative playing heads mentioned earlier in this chapter on membranophones. Before it can be mounted, the skin must first be soaked in water. Make sure that the skin is a little larger than the diameter of the pot to be used.

The rommelpot was a very popular instrument with singing beggars because to be able to play such an instrument demanded no musical talent whatsoever!

Twelfth Night was by far the best time to go from door to door with your rommelpot. In the illustration at the foot of the centre column, one of the musicians is playing a clog fiddle (pages 98-99).

Remove the bark from a thin length of elder wood and cut a notch near one end using a sharp hobby knife. Sandpaper the stick smooth and make sure there are no splinters or sharp edges. The stick should be roughly the same length as the pot.

The stick is fastened securely in the center of the drum skin (see illustration) with a length of strong thread.

Stretch the skin as tightly as possible over the top of the pot, making sure that the knotted end of the stick is inside the pot and therefore not visible to the eye.

Now fasten the skin firmly in place by wrapping thin cord several times around the pot and knotting it securely. The protruding edges of the skin can be cut off and the pot is then left for a few hours to dry out.

Playing the rommelpot

A lovely deep buzzing sound can be obtained by rubbing a damp cloth along the stick. Another method is to rub your wet hand up and down the stick or to rotate the stick slightly between the palms of the hands.

Traditionally, the rommelpot was played on Saint Martinmas or Twelfth Night and was accompanied by the lusty singing of traditional rommelpot songs.

These songs – like those sung to the accompaniment of a Hanske Knap – asked the listener to make a small contribution to the singers and players!

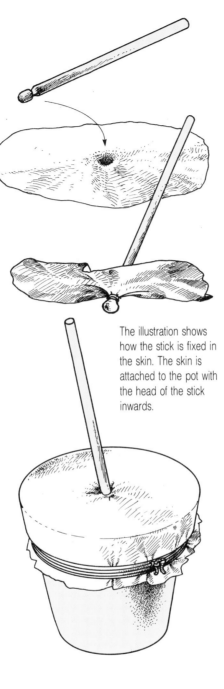

The illustration shows how the stick is fixed in the skin. The skin is attached to the pot with the head of the stick inwards.

The rommelpot song and fitting illustration.

I've wandered with my rommelpot all the livelong day
And I haven't got a penny a loaf of bread to buy
Mr Breadman, put a penny in my pocket, put a penny in my hat, I'd be very glad of that
Lady, will you let me in and open up the cookie tin?
Skipper, you must give your ground,
Skipper, you must haul your sails down,
Has anyone got a penny for the rommelpot?

The 'noneke' or mirliton

The 'noneke' also belongs to the family of membranophones because this instrument has a skin which is made to vibrate. This is achieved by blowing against it.

In days gone by the noneke was particularly favored by beggars – largely because it requires a minimum of talent to play! The noneke also requires a minimum of material (and expertise) to make! There is, however, ample opportunity to use your skill and imagination in decorating the instrument.

To make a mirliton all you need is a length of hollow wood or pipe with a hole burned or bored five centimetres from one end. A skin is stretched over that end with the aid of an elastic band. This can be an onion skin, a cigarette paper or a piece of thin plastic. An alternative mirliton can be made simply by folding a sheet of thin tissue paper over an ordinary comb!

A buzzing sound is produced by holding the flat side of the instrument against the lips humming over the skin.

A simple comb with a cigarette paper makes an excellent mirliton.

83

Chordophones

Chordophones are instruments in which the sound is produced by the vibrations of strings. There are five basic types of stringed instruments: bows, lyres, harps, lutes and zithers. The relationship of the strings to the body or resonator provides the usual means of classifying these instruments. For example, the string (or strings) of a musical bow — the simplest chordophone — is attached to the ends of a curved stick, while those of a zither are held away from the body by bridges.

Stringed instruments have a long and varied history. The musical bow is the oldest and simplest form of stringed instrument, but is still in regular use in Africa and America. Harps and lyres were first played some 5000 years ago in Egypt and Sumeria. Bows were first applied to the lute in the tenth century, and from this bowed lute developed the modern-day violin. Nowadays, music without stringed instruments is simply unthinkable — after all, what would a symphony orchestra be without its violins? And who can imagine a pop group without guitars?

'How do I earn a crust – 1900?' With a hurdy gurdy, of course! A London street scene around the turn of the century.

A 'matchstick' violin in which the soundbox is built entirely from matches glued together.

Chordophones

Stringing

As already mentioned in the introduction to this chapter, chordophones are classified according to the way in which the strings are attached to the instrument.

The musical bow (A) in the most simple stringed instrument and consists of a curved stick with the string(s) attached to both ends. The lyre (B) consists of a resonator or soundbox and the strings run from this to a crossbar supported by two arms.

The resonator amplifies the sound. The strings of the harp (C) run at an oblique angle from the resonator to the neck, while the strings of the lute (D) run from near the base of the body, over a bridge, to the end of the neck. Zither strings (E) run along the whole length of the instrument, parallel to the body. They are lifted away from the body by means of bridges.

Stringing

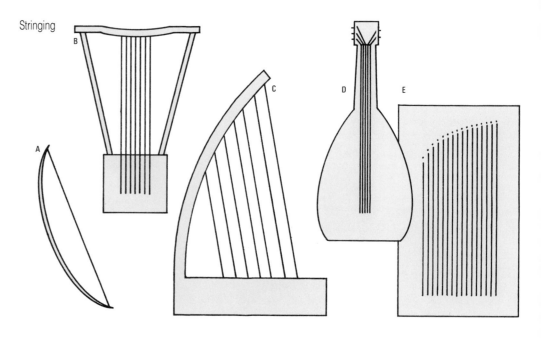

Lifting the strings

In order to vibrate freely, the strings of lyres, lutes and zithers must be lifted from the body. This can be achieved in different ways.

If the strings are attached directly to the body, they can be lifted by means of a bridge (A). Strings are sometimes attached to a string holder (or tailpiece) which acts as a bridge and lifts the strings clear of the body (B).

Attaching the strings

The strings of chordophones can be attached to the instrument in various ways.

The simplest method is to attach them directly to the neck (A) but the great disadvantage of this is that the instrument is then very difficult to tune.

The instrument is much easier to tune if the strings are attached to a tuning ring (B) or a wooden tuning pin (C).

Sounding the strings

Chordophones can be played in a number of different ways. Most common are plucking – with the fingers (A) or a plectrum (B) – and bowing (C).

Various types of zither are played with sticks or hammers (D). The aeolian harp is unique in that it is played by one of nature's 'musicians' – the wind!

Lifting the strings

Attaching the strings

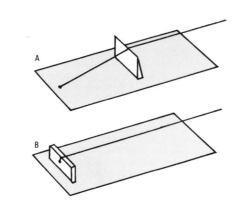

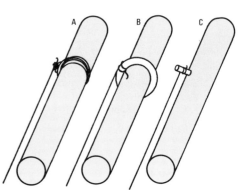

Sounding the strings

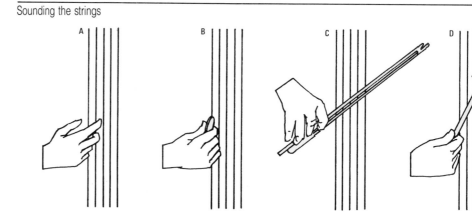

How a string vibrates

An activated string vibrates not only as a whole but also in sections, as shown in the diagram. The longest vibration – the 'primary vibration' determines the pitch produced. This is called the fundamental.

The shorter vibrations – the 'secondary vibrations' produce harmonics or overtones which sound in conjunction with the fundamental. These overtones give each instrument its own particular sound. By touching a string very lightly with the finger while bowing normally, a harmonic is obtained in place of the fundamental.

Strings and pitch

Pitch is determined by the length, thickness and tension of the string. A short string gives a higher pitch than a long one (A).

A string at high tension gives a higher pitch than one which is less taut (B) and a thin string gives a higher pitch than a thick one (C).

Raising the pitch

From the foregoing it is clear how the pitch can be altered – a pitch can be raised by shortening the vibrating length of the string or lowered by increasing the length. When playing this is usually achieved by 'stopping' the string – pressing it against the neck or body of the instrument (A). Some instruments have frets (B) – very low bridges on the neck or body which show the player where the string must be stopped.

Many zithers have movable bridges which can be adjusted to give the string a particular vibrating length and thus a particular pitch (C).

Resonators

A resonator or soundbox reinforces and amplifies the tone produced by the vibrating strings. Devices like the violin soundpost help spread the vibrations.

How a string vibrates

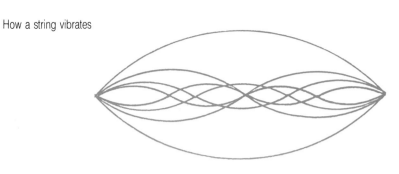

Strings and pitch

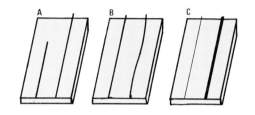

Raising the pitch

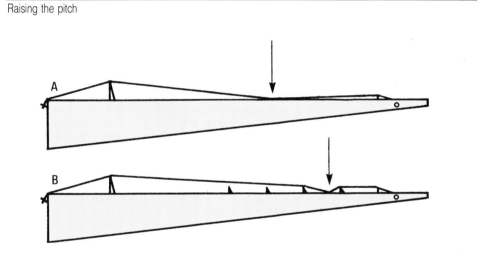

Resonators

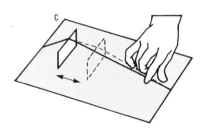
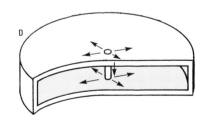

The musical bow (the bladder bow)

The simplest form of the musical bow is a curved stick with strings. Resonators were added later in order to modulate and strengthen the sound. The resonator of the instruments described here is a pig's or cow's bladder. The vibration is produced by means of a bow. This instrument can be compared to a tea chest bass which, apart from the resonator, is almost identical to it. The musical bow is a bourdon instrument, which means that it can only produce a basic tone. This, in turn, means that the musical bow is an excellent accompanying instrument, an instrument which was already very popular some hundreds of years ago.

The hole for the tuning pin is drilled at right angles to this and then slightly tapered with a conical gouge. The tuning pin is cut roughly and then 'sharpened' with a conical sharpener (see Tools, page 8) so that it fits tightly into the hole. The fret – which prevents the string cutting into the neck – is positioned as indicated in the illustration. This is made by bending a length of 2 mm wire into a U-shape. To mount the fret, drill two small holes, add a little glue to the ends and tap it carefully into place. The string clamps the bladder in place and is attached to the tuning pin and to the end of the neck behind the bladder.

Making a musical (bladder) bow

To make this instrument you need a long neck, a string, a dressed (cleaned) pig's or cow's bladder and a bow.
The bladder is soaked for five minutes in warm water. It is then inflated and tied off with string. It is also possible to fit the bladder with a valve from a bicycle innertube so that it can be easily reinflated. You need a cork or wood stop the same size as the bladder opening. Drill a hole through the center of the stop, position the valve over this hole and fold the surrounding rubber innertube over it. The whole is then glued in the bladder opening and tightly fastened with strong thread (see the illustration). Use a plane, rasp and sandpaper to shape the neck as shown in the illustration. The long oval hole at the end of the neck is made by boring two large holes in the positions indicated and then cutting out the surplus wood with a keyhole saw.

One version of a self-made musical bow. The soundbox consists of a dressed inflated cow's bladder. The sound is produced with a bow.

Bells can be attached in order to accentuate the rhythm, but are not really necessary.

The finished instrument can be decorated in a variety of ways. Patterns can be carved or branded into the neck, for example, or colored ribbons can be tied to its ends. Small bells, metal disks or strings of shells or beads can also be attached to the instrument and these add an extra dimension to the sound produced.

The bow

You can also make the bow with which this instrument is played. The best material for the string is tail hair obtained from a stallion, although very strong cotton thread can be used instead. The strings are well-rubbed with violin resin which can be bought in a music store.

A piece of willow, approximately 60 cm in length, is used for the bow. A hole is bored in the thicker end and a notch cut in the thinner end. The strings can then be attached as shown in the illustration.

A detail from the 'Festival of Fools' by Pieter Brueghel the Elder. A musical bow can be seen in the top right hand corner.

600

A simple bow can be made out of a willow branch and a length of cotton thread.

The illustration shows how the tuning pin and neck are built. If the bladder tends to lose air, it can be fitted with a cap containing a valve from a bicycle innertube. This valve is held in place by strong thread.

Playing the musical bow

The musical bow is a typical accompanying instrument and is not suitable for playing melodies.

The string is made to vibrate by stroking it with the bow. Set the end of the neck on top of your foot and stamp the rhythm as you play. Bells attached to the instrument heighten the rhythmic effect.

The pitch can be altered by stopping the string with the thumb or fingers of the hand in which the instrument is held.

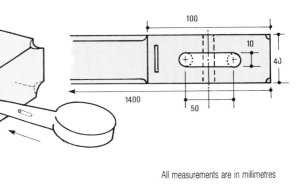

100

10

40

1400

50

All measurements are in millimetres

89

The talharpa

The talharpa (or tallharpa), which literally means 'bowed harp', was originally a Swedish instrument but it is still made and played in the Soviet Republic of Estonia and in Karelia. These stringed instruments appeared in Sweden, Finland and Russia during the Middle Ages and are one of the few types which have managed to survive over the centuries. As in western Europe troubadors and bards traveled around to festivals and courts, so in this area of Russia players wandered with their talharpas from one feast or wedding party to another. Usually all they earned was a place to sleep and and few glasses of gin. (See also page 119).

The talpharpa is made from a block of pine or lime measuring 140×570×60 mm. Draw the shape of the soundbox and arms on the wood according to the dimensions given in the illustration. Cut out the arms using a small handsaw or tenon saw and a keyhole saw. The crosspiece – the tuning pin holder – will be glued to these arms at a later stage.

The talharpa – a type of bowed lyre – was played during wedding parties and other festivities in Estonia and Karelia. The strings were made from the tail hair of the stallion. This model has a missing string.

90

The soundbox

The block of wood is hollowed out using a gouge and chisel. The walls should be as thin as possible (c. 4-5 mm), because the thinner the walls, the greater the volume of the soundbox – and the greater the volume of the soundbox, the more beautiful the tone it produces! Take great care during the last phase to avoid breaking through the wood! The crosspiece, or tuning pin holder, is made from a piece of pine or lime measuring 25×140×34 mm. Cut away the bottom corners as indicated in the illustration. Bore four equidistant holes, 9 mm in diameter, from top to bottom. These should be bored at an angle so that the tuning pins lock when the strings are tensioned. The finished tuning pin holder is now glued to the arms of the soundbox. The top of the talharpa is slightly curved (see center illustration). Remove the surplus wood along the sides with a plane or rasp and then sand the surface smooth. The bottom edges and all the corners are also rounded. The upper panel consists of a sheet of pine or lime measuring 140×440×3 mm. The grain must run along the length of the instrument. Cut two sound holes in the panel (in principle they can be any shape you wish) using a fretsaw. Heat the inner side of the panel with a smoothing iron – this will cause it to bow – and glue it to the soundbox. When the glue has dried, remove any remnants and sandpaper the edges. A drawer knob is glued and screwed in the middle of the back of the soundbox. The string holder will be attached to this later.

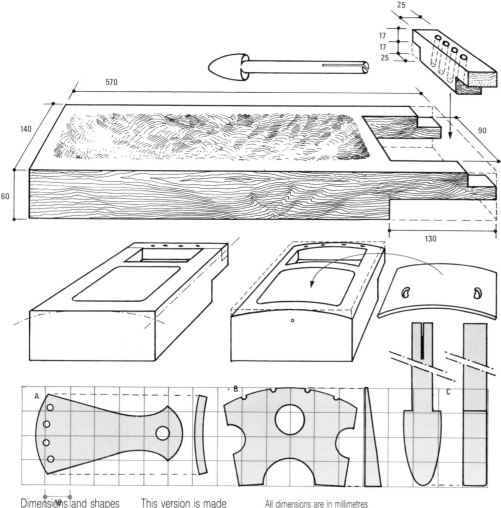

Dimensions and shapes are given in the upper illustration.

This version is made from one hollowed-out piece of wood.

All dimensions are in millimetres

instrument. Clamp the pins in a vise and cut broad notches, approximately 35 mm deep, in the ends of the pins – these will anchor the strings. Give the pins a final rub down with sandpaper and mount them in the holes in the crosspiece.

The strings
The strings are made from the tail hair of a stallion or a gelding. Tail hair derived from a mare is not suitable. When a mare passes water, she tends to foul her tail and this stiffens the hair. If there is no riding school or friendly farmer in your neighbourhood, this hair can also be bought at a music store. If necessary, nylon thread can be used.

Twist a bundle of hair to form a string and knot this to the string holder, clamping the other end in the notch of the tuning pin. Repeat this operation for the other strings and then fix the string holder to the knob at the back of the sound box with a thin cord. The bridge is held in position (see model) by the tension of the strings. This tension is achieved by twisting the tuning pins.

Making the bow
The bow is made from a length of meranti or some similar hardwood measuring 2×1×55 cm. Cut out the shape – as shown in the model – using a jigsaw or fretsaw. Round off the bow using a fine rasp and sandpaper. Bore a hole 2 mm in diameter in each end. Knot the bundle of horsehair in each hole. The hair at the end which is held is wrapped in strips of cotton cloth tied in place with thin cord. When playing, the bow string is tensioned by pressing this tight with the fingers.

Playing the talharpa
The talharpa is played with a bow. You can make this yourself – as described above – or you can buy one for a few dollars in a music store.

Take the neck of the instrument between the thumb and index finger of the left hand. Now apply pressure to the two upper strings with the middle and ring fingers. By increasing and decreasing the pressure the pitch is respectively raised and lowered. The two lower strings function as bourdons and do not change in pitch (for stringing see also page 119).

String holder and bridge
The string holder (A) is made of hardwood such as maple or meranti. Enlarge, transfer and cut out the shape. Note that the holder is slightly rounded. The original piece should be cut some 3 mm thicker than required and then rounded with a rasp and gouge. Drill holes in the positions indicated in the illustration – four 1 mm holes for the strings and a 2 mm hole for the cord which attaches it to the body. The bridge (B) is also made from maple. Enlarge, transfer and cut out the bridge using a fretsaw. (Shapes other than that illustrated can be made, of course.) As the illustration shows, one side of the bridge is tapered. When the bridge is in place, this side faces the tuning pins. The cord which attaches the string holder in position can easily cut into

the soft pine or lime panel of the soundbox. This can be prevented by inserting a thin piece of a harder wood, (beech or plum, for example) or bone in the upper edge of the panel. Carefully chisel a piece 20 mm wide and 2 mm deep from the edge and glue in the replacement piece of hardwood or bone.

The tuning pins
The four tuning pins (C) are cut from a piece of scrap hardwood. They should be 9 mm in diameter and 9.5-10 cm in length. Work them into shape with a fine file and sandpaper. They should fit snugly in the holes in the tuning pin holder. Make sure that the flat ends of the pins are broad enough to give the fingers enough leverage to twist the pin easily while tuning the

The African lyre

In contrast to the European lyre (which is bowed), the African lyre is a member of the plucked lyre family. Long ago, these lyres were found all over the world, but nowadays they are only seen in Africa and in some parts of Siberia. Lyres which have a bowl-shaped soundbox are the most commonly found. Those with box-shaped resonators are nowadays only found in Ethiopia. There are many types of African lyre – the bagana (a lyre for the nobility and priests), the kerar (a folk lyre), the obukano (an East African double bass) and the kissar, for example. The instruments are often decorated with skins, beads and feathers and are sometimes carved and painted.

An example of an African lyre. The resonator is a gourd covered with stretched animal skin.

A native of Sudan playing an African lyre. The strummed lyre is only found in African and Siberian cultures. African lyres are usually used as an accompaniment during magical and religious festivals.

Making the African lyre

The frame for the soundbox of the African lyre is made in the same way as that for the frame drum and tambourine.
You need a mold or template, a length of plywood and (at a later stage) two drum skins. To make the frame, follow the instructions given for the frame drum on page 80.

Three holes, 28 mm in diameter, are bored where indicated in the illustration using a 28 mm auger. (Take care no to split the frame when boring these holes.)

The arms and crosspiece
The arms consist of two rounded lengths of wood, 700 mm in length and with a diameter of 28 mm. Broom handles are quite suitable. Cut one end of each length diagonally, as indicated in the illustration. The pieces are now inserted through the two adjacent holes, the diagonally-cut ends meeting in the third hole and protruding slightly through it.
A hole is now bored approximately 30 mm from the end of each arm using a 14 mm auger. These holes should be parallel to the soundbox and are therefore at a slight angle to the arm itself (see the illustration).

The crosspiece is a round length of wood with a diameter of 14 mm and a length of approximately 500 mm. Cut it to the exact length plus 2×10 cm. Three holes, 50 mm apart, are drilled in the center of the crosspiece. These should have a diameter of 4.5 mm and are intended for the tuning pins. Use an awl to make 'starter' holes so that the drill does not slip.
Using a good quality wood glue, glue the ends of the arms together in the third hole and the crosspiece in the two arms. The holes for the tuning pins run at an angle from front to back so that the pins themselves are set diagonally (see illustration within the dotted circle).

93

The tuning pins

The tuning pins are made as follows: take three pieces of soft steel 5 cm in length and 5 mm in diameter. The end 15 mm of each piece is beaten flat on both sides – do this on a heavy metal plate using a peen hammer. At the foot of this flat section bore a 1 mm hole using a steel drill. Make a 'starter' hole with a punch so that the drill does not slip. The pins can then be tempered by placing them on a hotplate or in a hot open flame.

The skins

Skins are now stretched over both sides of the soundbox. These should be mounted, while wet, with large round-headed panel pins (see tambourine). You can also apply the principle used for the frame drum and lace the two skins together with leather thongs or nylon cord.

The string holder and bridge

The string holder (A) is made from maple. Cut this out according to the illustration and drill four holes, 1 mm in diameter, in the indicated positions.

A screw-eye is screwed and glued into the ends of the arms protruding from the soundbox. The string holder is fixed to this screw-eye with strong nylon thread.

The bridge (B) is made from a piece of maple measuring $70 \times 40 \times 5$ mm. One side of the bridge is tapered with a smoothing plane (see illustration) and notches for the strings are cut into the top edge in the positions indicated. The bridge is held in the required position by the tensioned strings (see illustration).

For the strings use stallion or gelding tail hair, nylon thread or ready-made guitar strings. The strings are attached to the string holder and the tuning pins are tensioned and tuned by turning these pins.

Playing the African lyre

The African lyre is a plucked instrument and is played purely by ear. Every instrument is played differently depending on the tension of the strings.

The African lyre was mostly used to accompany the singing at religious feasts and magical rites.

The tuning key

In order to tension the tuning pins it is necessary to make your own tuning key. You need a piece of round soft steel approximately 80 mm in length and with a diameter of 6 mm. In one end cut a tapering notch 5 mm to 3 mm wide and 15 mm deep (see illustration page 96). Bend the steel at right angles at a distance of 3 cm from the notched end. The longer end is glued into a wooden handle. These can be bought for a dollar or so or you can use a handle from a file or an old pan. The key can be strengthened by glueing a length of copper tube – 20 mm in length and with an internal diameter of 6 mm – over the end. The finished tuning key is ideal for tuning other instruments such as the tin can banjo and the hummel.

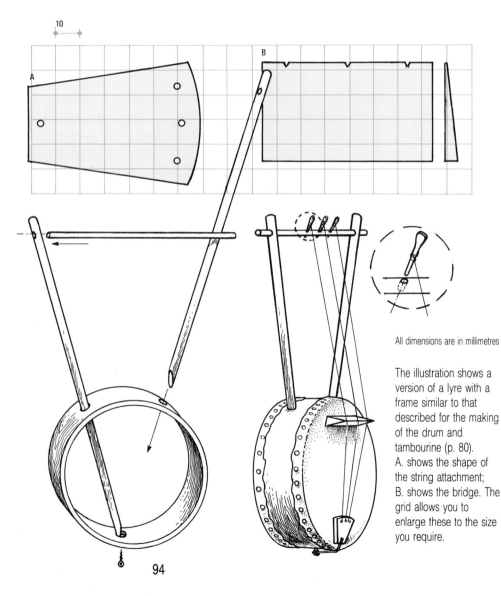

10

A

B

All dimensions are in millimetres

The illustration shows a version of a lyre with a frame similar to that described for the making of the drum and tambourine (p. 80). A. shows the shape of the string attachment; B. shows the bridge. The grid allows you to enlarge these to the size you require.

The tin can banjo

The banjo is a stringed instrument very popular in jazz bands, shows and revues, particularly in Britain and North America, and was developed from the long-necked lute which African slaves carried with them into captivity. As far as its dimensions are concerned, the traditional banjo is very much like the guitar, although the banjo has a relatively long neck, a circular soundbox and no sound holes. The tin can banjo described here is a folk instrument comparable to the South African ramkie (a folk guitar) ad is very easy to make. The soundboxes were originally made from gourds which had skins stretched over them. Nowadays, a simple tin can provides an excellent soundbox.

Although you might think the tin can banjo does not look like a 'real' musical instrument, you will quickly revise your opinion once you begin to play it!

Making the tin can banjo

For this banjo an ordinary, empty large tin can is used for the soundbox and a length of wood measuring 780×40×30 mm for the neck. The can is open at one end and should have no sharp edges.

A rectangle, measuring 40×30 mm, must be cut out just under the closed end. To do this use a can-opener or small, sharp kitchen or garden shears. The neck is now pushed through this hole until it reaches the far side of the can, where it is secured with glue or rubber cement and a round-headed screw. Rubber cement or glue is also smeared where the neck passes through the hole in the can. Any excess can be cleaned off later. The underside of the neck – to 150 mm from the end – is rounded off using a rasp and sandpaper. Three end pins are mounted in the end of the neck below the retaining screw. These are 10 mm apart and can be ordinary screws. Above the three end pins, bend the rim of the tin over to the center so that the sharp edge cannot cut into the strings.

The bridge and the end fret

The bridge is glued in the middle of the closed end of the can. It is made from a piece of hardwood or bone, triangular in cross-section, measuring 60×20×6 mm. Three grooves, 10 mm apart, are cut into the apex of the triangle (see the illustration overleaf). The end fret can be made from the same materials as the bridge and runs across the full width of the neck (40 mm). It also has three grooves at 10 mm distances.

The tin can banjo is a self-made version of a professional banjo and is made from a simple tin can. This produces a sound which is very close to the authentic banjo sound.

It can also be made in the same way as the other frets (see the following paragraph and illustration). The scale of this banjo – the length of the free vibrating strings – is 548 mm. The end fret is therefore positioned at a distance of 548 mm from the bridge.

The frets

The frets are positioned on the neck at the distances shown in the illustration. They are made from 2 mm steel wire and are a little narrower than the neck itself – 25-28 mm. Bend 45-48 mm lengths of wire in U-forms using a pair of pliers. Mark lines across the neck to indicate the positions of each fret and make starter holes with an awl. Drill holes 2 mm in diameter and 1 cm in depth – mark the drill 1 cm from the end with adhesive tape or a dab of paint. The frets are now tapped home using a light hammer.

Tuning pins

The simplest way to tension the strings is to mount three ready-made tuning keys at the end of the neck; this is explained under the heading 'Alternative tuning keys'. First we will explain how you can make and mount your own tuning pins.

To mount the tuning pins, three holes must be drilled in the end of the neck. These should have a diameter which is 0.5 mm less than that of the pins themselves. To make the pins you require three 40 mm lengths of soft steel, 5 mm in diameter.

Flatten the end 15 mm of each piece using a peen hammer. Immediately below the flattened end, drill a hole 1 to 1.5 mm in diameter (first

Chordophones

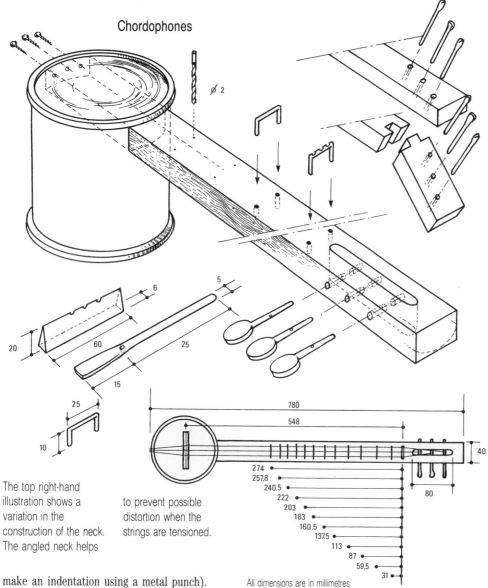

6

5

20

60

25

15

25

10

780

548

274
257.8
240.5
222
203
183
160.5
137.5
113
87
59.5
31

40

80

The top right-hand illustration shows a variation in the construction of the neck. The angled neck helps

to prevent possible distortion when the strings are tensioned.

All dimensions are in millimetres

in two ways – striking the strings and plucking. Some players use a metal or plastic plectrum, others mount various plectra on the ends of their fingers.

Playing is relatively simple with only three strings. The A, E and D chords are very easy to learn – no matter what tuning you have chosen for your banjo.

You will be amazed how many melodies you can play using only these three simple chords! Buy a handbook from a music store and learn additional cords.

The tuning key

In order to tension the tuning pins it is necessary to make your own tuning key. You need a piece of soft round steel approximately 80 mm in length and with a diameter of 6 mm. In one end cut a tapering notch 5 mm to 3 mm wide and 15 mm deep (see illustration below). Bend the steel at right angles at a distance of 3 cm from the notched end. The longer end is glued into a wooden handle. These can be bought for a dollar of so or you can use a handle from a file or an old pan.

The key can be strengthened by glueing a length of copper tube 20 mm in length and with an internal diameter of 6 mm – over the end. The finished tuning key is ideal for tuning other instruments such as the African lyre and the hummel.

make an indentation using a metal punch). The tuning pins can now be given a lovely, blueish gloss by heating them for a time in an open fire or on an electric hotplate – make sure they have cooled off completely before attempting to position them in the neck! The holes for the tuning pins are 22 mm deep and have a diameter of 4.5 mm. They must be drilled at an angle to the neck (see illustration). Gently tap the pins in position using a light hammer.

Alternative tuning keys

In the model shown in the photograph the builder has used a ready-made set of keys designed for the guitar.

A long, narrow hole must first be cut in the neck. The end of this hole is 50 mm from the end of the neck and it measures 10×80 mm. Mark it out on the neck and drill vertical

holes at each end using a 10 mm drill. Cut out the surplus wood using a keyhole saw and a gouge. Sand the inside smooth. Drill three 9 mm holes at 30 mm intervals through the side of the neck and mount the tuning key assembly.

Use a half-set of guitar strings for your banjo. These are knotted to the screwheads set in the back of the can and held by the tuning pins or keys. The banjo is tuned by tensioning these strings.

Finally, fix a strap so that you can hang the banjo around your neck while playing.

Playing the banjo

A banjo is a plucked stringed instrument, closely related to the ukelele. It can be played

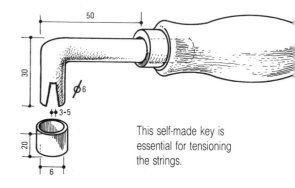

50

30

$\emptyset$ 6

3-5

20

6

This self-made key is essential for tensioning the strings.

The long-necked lute

Since the early Middle Ages there have been — generally speaking — two types of lute: the long-necked lute and the short-necked lute. Different forms developed in different regions — the bouzouki in Greece, the p'ip'a in China, the sitar in India and the balalaika in Russia, for example. The long-necked lute described here is a relative of the rebec, an instrument whose history can be traced back to Arabic lutes of the eleventh century.

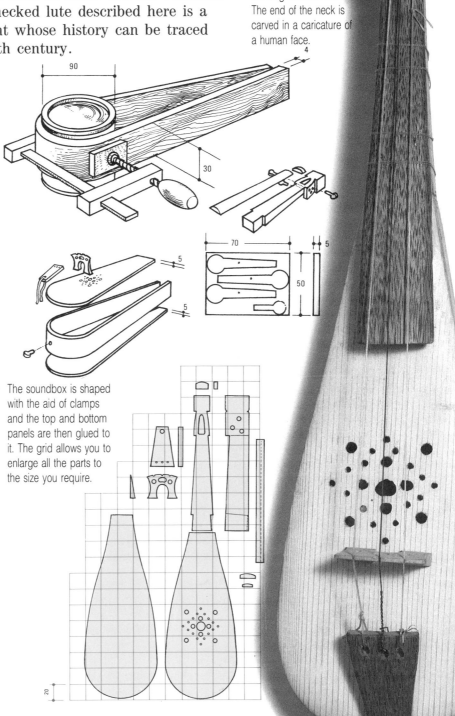

A self-made version of the long-necked lute. The end of the neck is carved in a caricature of a human face.

The soundbox is shaped with the aid of clamps and the top and bottom panels are then glued to it. The grid allows you to enlarge all the parts to the size you require.

Making the soundbox of the lute

Lutes exist in almost every conceivable shape and size, but all lutes have two things in common — the neck and soundbox resonate and the strings run from the string holder (which is fixed close to the bottom of the soundbox) along the full length of the neck. The instrument described here is approximately 400 mm in length. For the soundbox you first need a piece of pine 520 mm long, 35 mm wide and approximately 4 mm thick. This should be put into boiling water for five minutes or so — to make it flexible — and molded around a tin can, holding it in place with a clamp (see illustration). Allow the wood to dry thoroughly.

The upper and lower panels of the soundbox are cut from a sheet of pine measuring 200×230×5 mm. Lay the formed U-shape on the sheet of wood, draw round it with a pencil and cut out the two panels using a fretsaw. Drill and/or cut soundholes in the upper panel. Glue the panels in position and remove any surplus glue after is has dried. Round off the soundbox slightly using a rasp and sandpaper it smooth.

Making the neck

To make the neck use a piece of hardwood measuring 150×30×30 mm. Suitable woods include walnut and meranti. Cut the shape of the neck following the illustration using a fretsaw and tenon saw.

Round off the underside with a rasp and sand the whole neck smooth. Mark the position of the long oval hole for the tuning pins, drill 9 mm holes at each end and remove the surplus wood using a fretsaw and gouge. The head is shaped and decorated according to the illustration (or to a shape of your own preference) using a saw and chisel. In the past, all sorts of designs were used for the heads of lutes and these often represented the personal 'signature' of the builder.

Three holes, with a diameter of 4.5 mm, are drilled through the side of the neck to accommodate the tuning pins. These are then 'opened' using a conical gouge. The neck is now glued and screwed into the open, narrow end of the soundbox.

Making the bridge, string holder and tuning pins

The bridge and string holder are made from maple. Use the grid under the illustration to enlarge these pieces to the required size and cut them out using a fretsaw. Drill and cut the holes in the positions indicated.

Three tuning pins and an end pin are cut from a piece of hardwood measuring 50×70×5 mm, using a fretsaw (see illustration) and shaped using a conical sharpener (see Tools, page 8). A hole, 1 mm in diameter, is drilled in the middle of each of the three tuning pins (but not the end pin). All the pins are rounded and smoothed using a rasp and sandpaper. Finally a rounded tapered 'keyboard' (see illustration), made from a 200×30×5 mm piece of meranti, is glued along the neck and over the soundbox. Glue a protruding end fret in front of the hole for the tuning pins. The strings (use violin strings) are knotted to the string holder and threaded through the holes in the tuning pins. Finally the lute is tuned by tensioning the strings. The bridge is not attached to the soundbox but held in place by the strings.

Playing the lute

The lute is usually plucked with the fingers but it can also be played with a plectrum. The string vibrates from the bridge to the position where the string ends or to where it is stopped by a finger. By stopping the strings in this way it is possible to produce various pitches from a simple three-stringed lute.

The clog fiddle

Since very early times, both rich and poor alike have made music and built music instruments. It is only during the last few centuries that a difference between instruments for the rich and instruments for the poor has existed.

For the rich were the Stradivarius, Amati, Guarneri and Montagnana violins; for the poor in the Low Countries there were the 'stekskes' fiddle (made of matches) and the clog fiddle!

In fact the clog fiddle was the first instrument ever played by a number of well-known Flemish musicians and composers (such as Paul Gilson and Servais).

Making the fiddle

When making a clog fiddle you naturally start with a clog! It does not matter whether this is a clog for the right foot or the left – simply find the biggest you can lay your hands on! Saw the upper side straight off to the instep. Gouge out the inner walls

(carefully!) so that they are as thin as possible. The thinner the wall, the larger the volume of the soundbox – and the larger the volume of the soundbox, the lovelier the sound it produces. Sand the inner wall smooth. The upper panel is made from quarter-sawn pine, 3 mm in thickness. Turn the clog upside down, lay it on the wood and draw round it carefully. Cut out the panel and mark the positions of the bridge and the sound hole on its top surface. The bridge must be exactly in the center – otherwise it is not possible to bow the two outer strings alone without touching the side of the clog. The sound hole(s) are cut out using a fretsaw. These can vary in shape, but it is a good idea to continue the clog motif (see the blue shaded shapes in the illustration on page 100).

The soundpost must be positioned before the top panel is glued in position. This is a piece of dowel approximately 8 mm in diameter. It is clamped between the upper panel and the clog sole and helps spread the vibrations. The upper end of the soundpost lies directly behind one of the legs of the bridge. The lower end lies in a hole (1-2 mm deep and 8 mm in diameter) drilled into the inner sole of the clog. The length of the soundpost is thus the distance between the sole and upper panel, plus 1-2 mm. Position the soundpost and carefully glue the upper panel to the clog – making sure the soundpost remains in its position and does not fall or move. Sand all the edges.

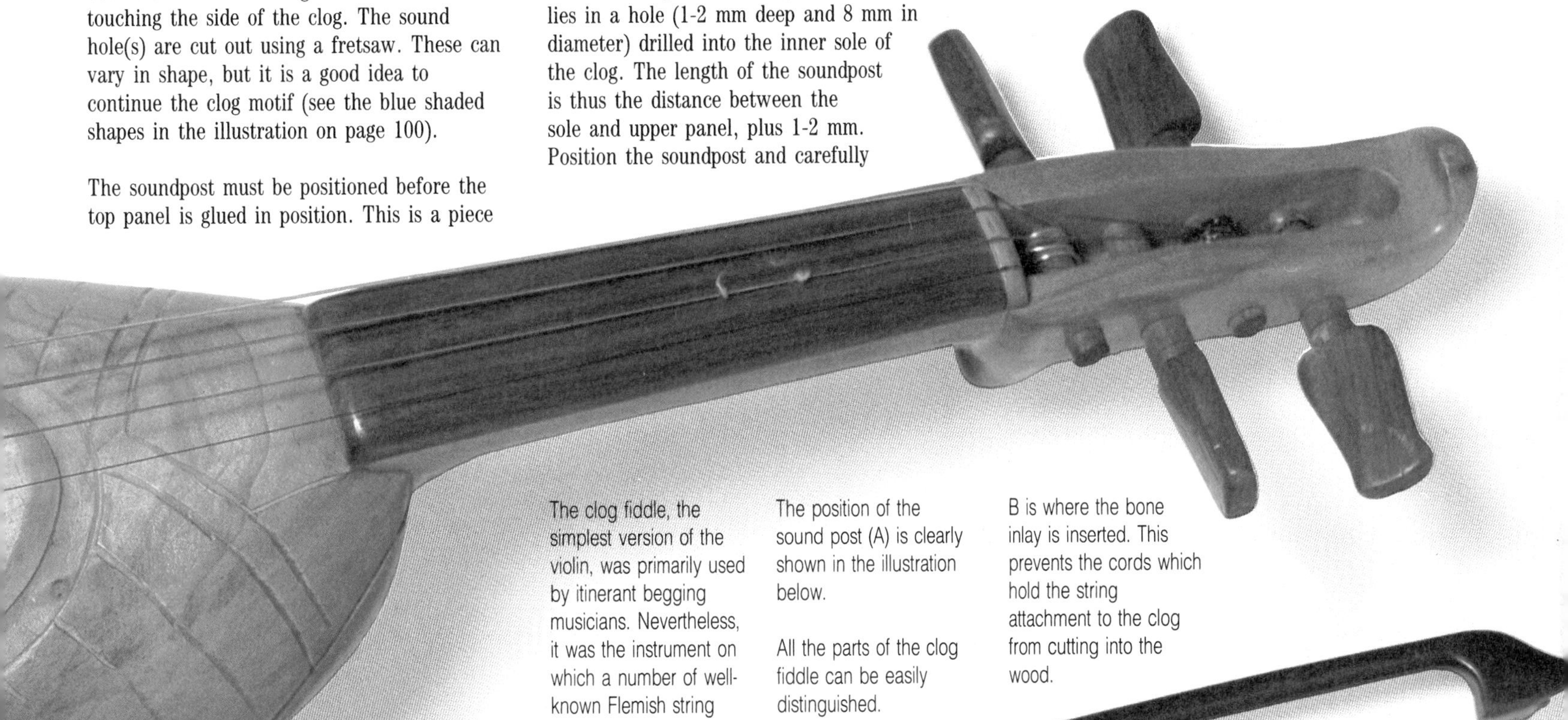

The clog fiddle, the simplest version of the violin, was primarily used by itinerant begging musicians. Nevertheless, it was the instrument on which a number of well-known Flemish string players and composers learned to play.

The position of the sound post (A) is clearly shown in the illustration below.

All the parts of the clog fiddle can be easily distinguished.

B is where the bone inlay is inserted. This prevents the cords which hold the string attachment to the clog from cutting into the wood.

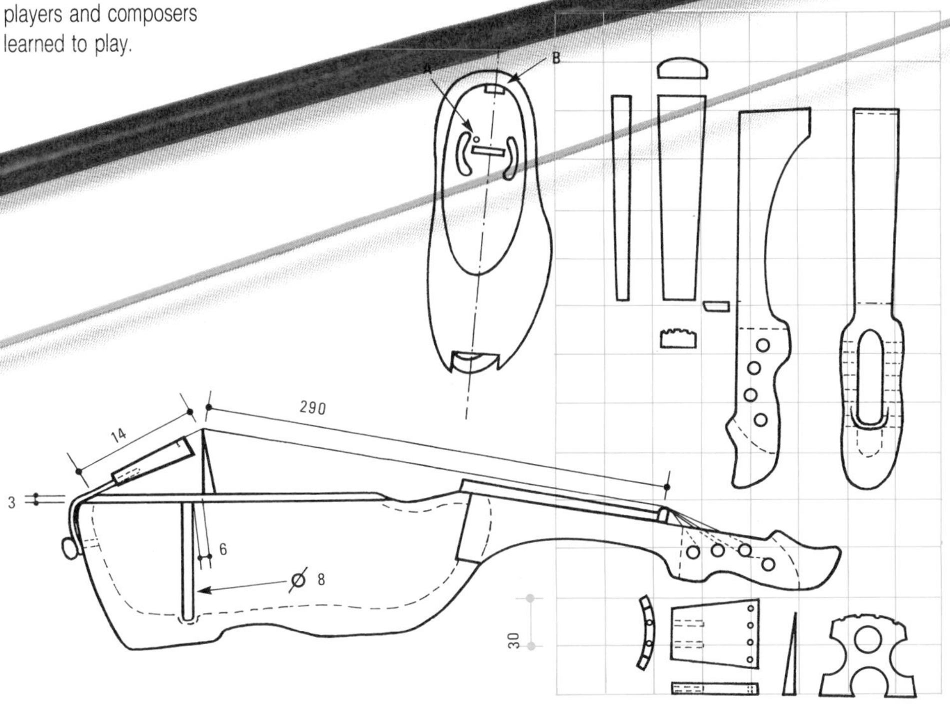

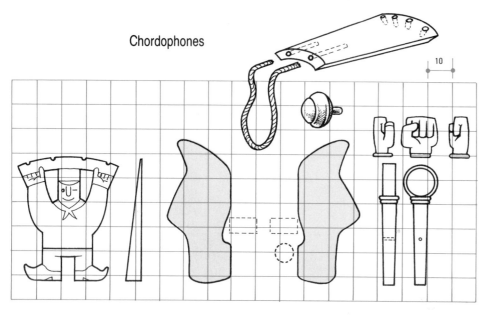

To add authenticity to your instrument, the bridge can be made in the form of a farmer, the sound hole in the shape of a clog, the tuning pins as hands.

The broken rectangles and circle show the position of the bridge and soundpost in relation to the sound hole.

The neck and head of the fiddle

The fiddle neck is cut from a block of hardwood (maple, pear, apple or plum) measuring 235×35×40 mm (see illustration on page 99) and shaped using a chisel, rasp and sandpaper.

A 'keyboard' of ebony or walnut is glued to the upper side of the neck. This keyboard is 28 mm wide and 6 mm thick at the head and 35 mm wide and 8 mm thick at the clog and can slightly overlap the toe.

The traditional head of the clog fiddle is also in the form of a clog and can be shaped using a rasp and sandpaper. (Some makers prefer to adhere to the more usual scroll form for the head.)

A hole, 85×18 mm, is cut to contain the tuning pins. First drill several holes and then remove the surplus wood using a fretsaw and gouge. Sand the inside smooth. The four holes for the tuning pins are drilled through the sides of the head in the position shown in the illustration. These holes are conical in shape (use a conical gouge) and the pins are shaped to fit using a matching conical sharpener. Ready-made tuning keys can also be used (see: Tin can banjo, page 96).

The neck is mounted into the toe of the clog with a good quality wood glue. The hole is roughly sawn out and then worked with a chisel and fine rasp so that the neck fits exactly. Set the neck at a slight angle so that the strings cannot touch the body of the clog. The scale (the distance over which the strings are free to vibrate) — in this case from the bridge to the end fret — is 290 mm. This is the same as in a traditional violin.

The end fret, made from a piece of hardwood measuring 28×5×7 mm and having four notches 7 mm apart is fixed at the end of the keyboard (see illustration).

The bridge and string holder

The bridge is made from maple. Cut out the shape according to the illustration using a fretsaw. The height of the bridge is determined by the angle at which the neck is set — the strings must never come in contact with either the clog or neck. The legs of the bridge are only cut to size after the neck has been attached to the clog body. Check this with a length of cord (the strings are attached only in the last phase).

The bridge is held in position by the tension in the strings. It is essential that the angle which the bridge makes with the upper panel (at the neck end) is a right angle and the bridge is therefore tapered (see the illustration). The tension in the strings bends the top of the bridge. The notches in the top edge of the bridge are 11 mm apart.

The string holder is made from ebony, walnut or rosewood. Use a piece measuring 93×40×10 mm. Cut the shape according to the model in the illustration. Notice that the string holder is curved in shape. Four holes, 1 mm in diameter, are drilled at the wider end. Two deep holes are drilled into the narrower end. The cord which attaches the string holder to the body is glued into these holes. An end pin (this can be a drawer knob) is fixed in the heel (see the illustration). The edge of the clog above the end pin — where the strings pass over the heel — is cut away to a depth of 2 mm and a piece of hardwood or bone inserted. This prevents the strings cutting into the body of the clog.

The bow

The best-known violin makers employed their own bowmakers, but most of these have remained anonymous!

You can buy a bow in a music store for a few dollars or you can make your own as described for the talharpa on page 92.

Playing the clog fiddle

In contrast to the ordinary violin, the clog fiddle does not sit under the chin, but against the armpit. The instrument is therefore not clamped but pushed against the body. In practice this means that the violin can only be played in the first position, with the fingers close to the head, otherwise the instrument would fall out of the hand. Instruction books can be bought in a music store for a few dollars — these not only give you the basic fingering techniques but also show you how to tune the instrument.

The hummel (Swedish board zither)

The hummel is a centuries-old board zither, a type of instrument which is still a popular folk instrument in many countries. Originally, the hummel probably came from Asian culture. In the Far and Middle East, one finds instruments very much like the hummel – the Persian 'Ahn' and the Chinese 'Kin', for example. It may be, however, that the hummel is directly related to the 'monochord' of the Middle Ages.

Making the hummel

Hummels can be found in all shapes and sizes but the basic principle is always the same. In the illustration on page 104 four different methods of construction are shown. The one we have described is the fourth. In this instance, we are making a tenor hummel. The soprano, alto and bass models can easily be built using the information contained in the text and in the table on page 105. We begin with a solid block of hardwood measuring 825×105×34 mm. Various types of wood, such as walnut, cherry, beech and maple, can be used. A nice idea is to use different woods – for example, walnut for the soundbox and

The hummel is a member of the zither family. Most European zithers are board zithers and consist of a board or soundbox across which strings are stretched. Since medieval times, they have been associated with folk and religious music, often used to accompany hymn and psalm singing. The melody and chords are produced by pressing a wooden stave on the strings with the left hand. The strings are plucked with a plectrum held in the right hand.

A (rather rude) hummel song!

How do I creep into your room?
Where must I put my shoes and socks?
Where must I lay my working clothes?
How do I crawl into your bed?
Where must I put my tender toes?
What must I lay my hands upon?
Where should I stick my waggling tail?

maple for the upper panel. The side walls are 8 mm in thickness, the end wall approximately 20 mm and the sloping front 115 mm. Mark these dimensions on the surface of the block. Drill holes of 7 mm diameter at each corner, insert a jigsaw and cut out the middle section of the block. This can be used to make a smaller hummel – in this way you can make bass, tenor, alto and soprano hummels from one large initial block! In this model the dimensions of the bottom panel are 825×105 mm; for the bass and tenor the thickness is 4 mm, for the alto and soprano it is 3 mm. In all the models, the bottom panel is preferably of walnut, cherry, beech or maple. The front end (115 mm) is now sloped using a plane and a rasp (see illustration). The bottom panel should be glued to the frame as quickly as possible – the wood can 'work' if left too long. Fix the panel firmly to the frame with clamps and tape and set it aside for a few hours to dry at normal room temperature (approx. 20°C).

The next step is to make the upper panel. This measures 710×105×4 mm. The sound hole(s) – examples of which are given in the illustration (G) on page 105 – is cut out level with the last fret (between 480 and 490 mm from the end fret). Smooth the upper panel with sandpaper and give it a coat of instrument oil or varnish.

When the panel is dry the frets can be mounted in position. These are U-shaped and are made by bending 45-48 mm lengths of wire with a pair of pliers (or in a vise). The actual fret is 25-28 mm and each 'leg' is therefore 10 mm in length. You need 17 frets made from 1.5 mm wire and 2 made from 2 mm wire. The two thicker frets are those at the tuning pin end of the fret board (the end fret) and under the chord strings. Three and two grooves respectively are cut into these frets using a hacksaw (see illustration on page 105). Draw a line 8 mm from the side wall with a soft pencil and another line parallel to the first at a distance equal to the width of the frets. The fret positions are measured from the end fret and this is positioned exactly 50 mm from the tuning pin end of the upper panel. Use the table on page 105 to mark the position of each fret. Prick 'starter' holes with an awl and drill 1.5 mm holes (2 mm for the two end frets) for each fret. Now tap the frets into position. Turn the panel over and lay it on a

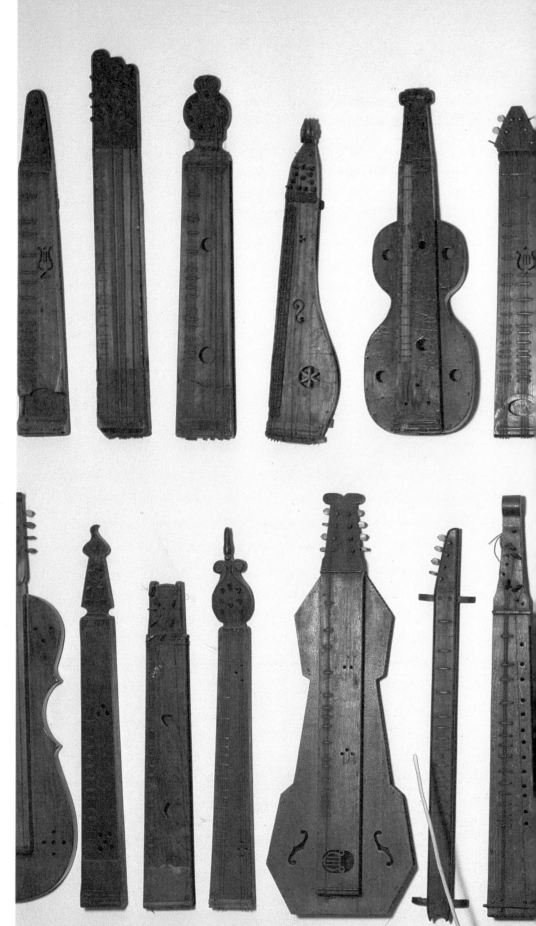

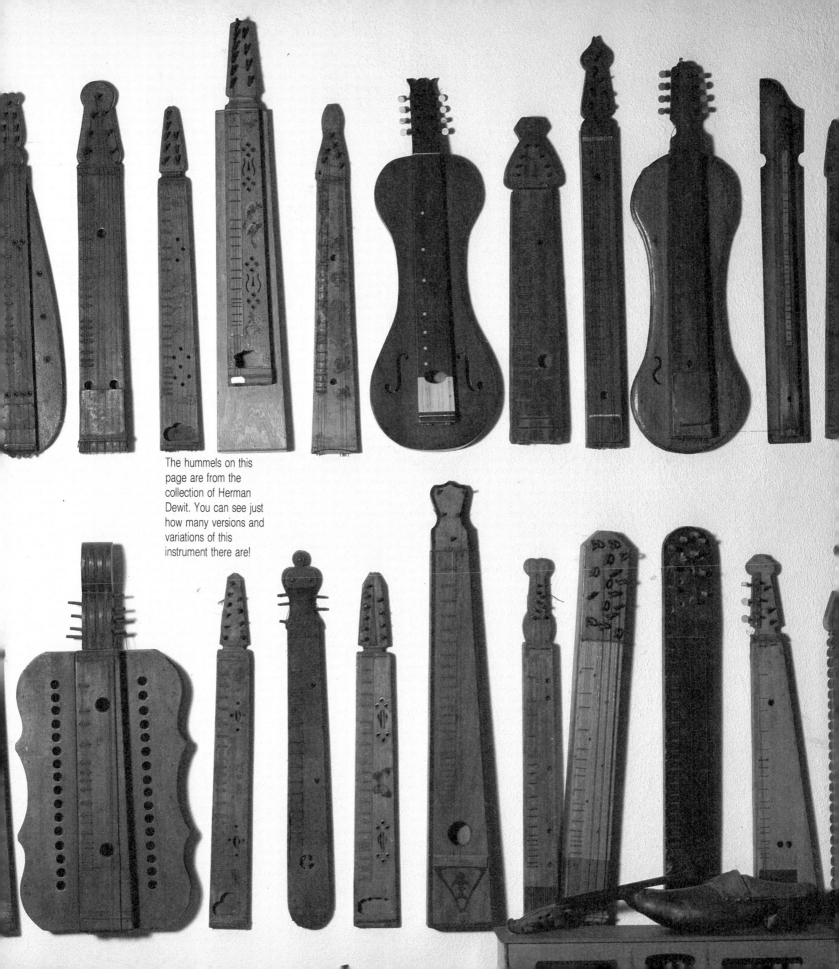

The hummels on this page are from the collection of Herman Dewit. You can see just how many versions and variations of this instrument there are!

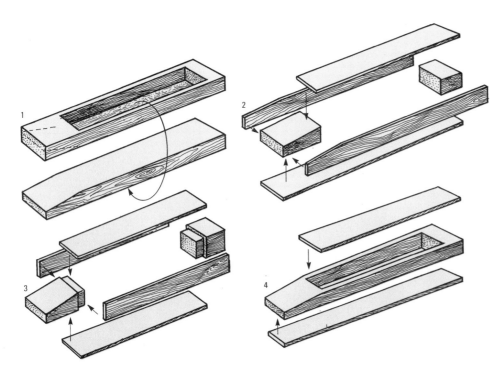

There are four methods of building a hummel. These are illustrated here. The version given in this book is that in which the soundbox is cut from a single piece of wood (this is version 4 in the diagram).

hard surface (a workbench or a metal plate, for example). Using a light hammer bend the legs over to fix the frets in position. The next step is to glue the upper panel to the soundbox. When the glue has dried, remove any remants and sandpaper the whole smooth. A plectrum can damage the upper panel and in order to prevent this a thin sheet of veneer can be glued over the last 140 mm or so (between the sound hole and the end of the panel). The grain of this veneer must run across the panel, not along its length. Sandpaper and give the instrument a coat of oil or varnish.

The bridge (see illustration page 105, A) is now made and mounted. This consists of a length of hardwood with a cross section of approximately 4×8 mm and is rounded off at the top back corner. The bridge runs over the full width of the soundbox and sits on the box itself. The front of the bridge is exactly 650 mm from the end fret. Mark the position of the bridge and cut a channel in the upper panel using a tenon saw and chisel. Glue the bridge in this channel and then cut notches for the strings in the positions indicated in the illustration.

The tuning pins and strings
The tuning pins are made from lengths of soft steel approximately 5 mm in diameter and some 40 mm in length. The last 15 mm of each pin is beaten flat with a peen hammer. At a distance of 15 mm from the other end of the pin a hole, 1 mm in diameter, is drilled. A 'starter' hole is first made using a metal punch – this prevents the drill slipping. The pins are tempered by holding them over an open flame or laying them on an electric hotplate for a short period of time. The holes for the tuning pins are now bored in the end of the soundbox. These should be about 24 mm deep and set at an angle (see illustration) so that the pins lock when the strings are tensioned. To make these holes use a drill which is 0.5 mm smaller than the diameter of the pins. Tap the tuning pins carefully into place. Note: the important point is that the hole in the pins (and therefore the strings) should be 1 to 1.5 mm above the upper panel when the pins are in place. Five pins or screws – three for the melody strings and two for the chord strings – are now mounted in the end of the sound box. These should be exactly in line with the tuning pins so that the strings lie parallel to each other (see illustration). Place these pins

at different heights in order to prevent the wood splitting. The hummel can now be stringed. Knot one end to the pins in the soundbox and the other through the holes in the tuning pins and then tension and tune the strings.

Making the playing stick
The hummel strings are pressed with a simple playing stick. Use a piece of hardwood about 10 cm in length and 15 mm in diameter. Use the grid in the illustration to enlarge the shape and mark it on the wood using an HB pencil. Cut out the stick using a fretsaw and shape it with a rasp and sandpaper. Varnish it.

Playing the hummel
You do not need a great deal of technique or experience to play the hummel. It is often used as a solo instrument but also sounds very good when played with other instruments or with one or more hummels. The hummel is played with two hands: with one hand you press the stick between two frets in order to produce different tones and with the other you pluck the strings between the bridge and the first fret.

The tuning key

A tuning key is an essential tool for tuning the hummel. These can sometimes be found in a music store but it is a simple matter to make your own. How to do this is described on page 94 and again on page 96 – where you will find an illustration.

All dimensions are in millimetres

A. shows the bridge. This is sunk through the upper surface and rests on the soundbox.
B. are the end frets and have respectively two and three grooves for the strings.
C. shows the frets and the manner in which they are fixed.
D. is the tuning pin made from a piece of steel. The tuning pins are tensioned with a specially-made tuning key (E).
F. is the playing stick
G. shows examples of sound holes.

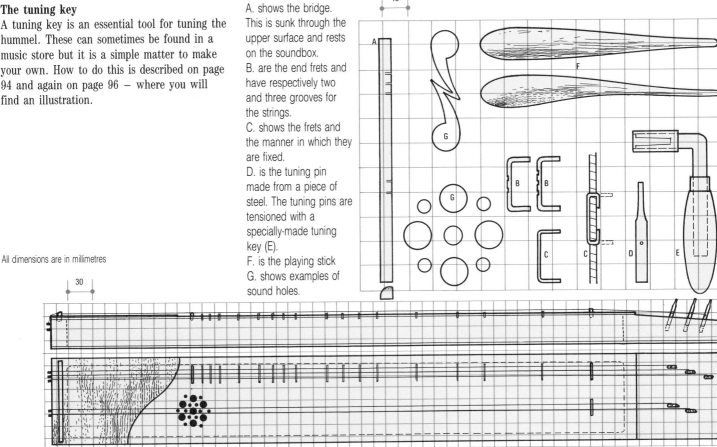

In order to prevent damage to the upper surface of the hummel while playing it is best to glue a thin sheet of hardwood veneer between the bridge and the sound hole. The grain of this veneer should lie across the length of the hummel.

This table shows the relative positions of the frets. The distances between the frets are determined by the length of the string between the end fret and the bridge. These lengths are 348 mm, 500 mm, 650 mm, and 848 mm, respectively, for a soprano, alto, tenor and bass hummel.

All fret positions are measured from the end fret.

	(soprano) 348 mm	Alto (500 mm)	Tenor (650 mm)	Bass (848 mm)
1st	-38 mm	-54.5 mm	-71 mm	-93 mm
2nd	-72	-103	-134	-175
3rd	-87.5	-125.5	-163	-213.3
4th	-115.3	-166.3	-215.8	-282.3
5th	-141	-202.8	-263.5	-344.3
6th	-152.5	-220	-285.3	-372.3
7th	-163.5	-235	-305.5	-399
8th	-174	-250	-325	-423.5
9th	-193	-277	-360.3	-470.3
10th	-201.3	-289.8	-377	-491.3
11th	-209.8	-301.5	-391.8	-511.3
12th	-217.5	-312.5	-406.5	-531.5
13th	-232	-333	-433	-565
14th	-244	-351	-456.8	-595.5
15th	-250.5	-359.5	-467	-610
16th	-256	-367.6	-478	-623
17th	-261	-375	-487.5	-636

The hurdy gurdy

The hurdy gurdy has been a well-known and much-loved instrument ever since the twelfth century. The earliest versions were for two players but in the course of the centuries the hurdy gurdy evolved into a practical stringed instrument for one player. The basic form of the instrument has not changed essentially since the seventeenth century and during the eigtheenth century it was very popular in the French royal court. Nowadays, the hurdy gurdy is mainly played at folklore festivals in France, Belgium, Hungary and Sweden, among other countries. The construction of the hurdy gurdy has fascinated instrument makers for centuries and building such a technically complex instrument quite clearly calls for considerable craftsmanship and manual skill. Potential builders be warned! An experienced hurdy gurdy maker requires a minimum of 160 hours to construct the instrument. Only begin, therefore, if you have indefatigable perseverence, two trusty right or left hands, a great deal of experience and the necessary tools!

The principle of the hurdy gurdy

The principle of the hurdy gurdy is actually very simple: A wooden disk, which protrudes through the upper panel of a soundbox, is turned by means of a handle. The wheel brushes against five strings – two bourdon strings, a trumpet string and two melody strings. The melody strings are played by pushing in a series of keys while the bourdon strings provide a continuous accompanying tone. The trumpet string produces not only a bourdon tone but also a rhythmical sound, depending on how fast the handle is turned.

A picturesque hurdy gurdy built by Hans Goddefroy, one of the authors of this book.

Hans and Mechel
Goddefroy in their
streetmusicians
costumes. The puppet is
attached to their legs by
cord and is made to
dance in time to the
music.

The hurdy gurdy model described in this chapter. It was designed and built by Herman Dewit, who is also one of the authors of this book.

Making a hurdy gurdy

Making a hurdy gurdy is highly exacting and painstaking work. Carefully study all the shapes and dimensions given in the illustrations and the instructions before you begin. Check each piece for fit before you finish it off – a small error quickly becomes a large one, however carefully you follow working drawings.

Only choose top quality wood (walnut) and always work with good, sharp tools. But be warned – you are taking on quite a task. We wish you the very best of luck!

The soundbox

The soundbox consists of a back panel, two side panels, a front panel, a bottom panel (or base) and an upper panel. The tuning pin box is at the front of the instrument, the handle is at the back. To begin with, the front panel, back panel, side panels and tuning pin box are made and assembled. The base and upper panel will be mounted at a later stage.

easiest way to do this is by means of a circular saw but a tenon saw and a 3 mm chisel can also be used. The sides of the panel are now rounded off using a rasp and sandpaper (see illustration). The upper and lower side of the panel should also be rounded using a plane, rasp and sandpaper (4).

The side panels

First make a template! The side panels are made from a sheet of walnut measuring 600×260×3 mm. Lay the template on the sheet and draw round it. Reverse the template

The back panel

First draw the shapes to the required size on sheets of cardboard, cut them out and use them as templates – *this applies to every part of the instrument.*

The back panel is made from a block of wood measuring 300×130×35 mm. Transfer the shapes to the wood. The outer side is rounded off using a plane, rasp and sandpaper (1).

The inner side is shaped by making a number of saw cuts to the curved lines and chiseling out the surplus wood. The surface is smoothed using a rasp and sandpaper (2).

Part of the center is also removed, leaving a 35×35 mm block at the top and one of 3×35 mm at the bottom (3).

A hole, 13 mm in diameter is bored at right angles through the center of the 35×35 mm block with an auger. This supports the wheel axis. The 3×35 mm block acts as support for the base.

A groove, 3 mm wide and 5 mm deep, is cut in each end of panel (see illustration). The

The top and inner views of the completed back panel.

Right: The back panel is made in four stages. You need a saw, chisel, plane, file and sandpaper.

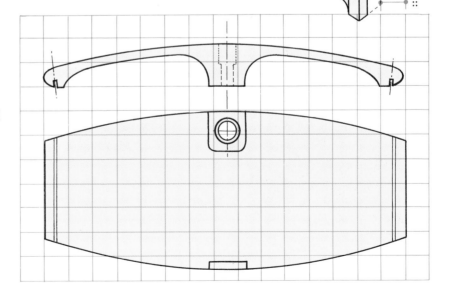

Chordophones

A typical hurdy gurdy built by the Dutch artist, Cornelis LeMair. He also painted the miniatures which decorate this model.

and draw round it again (one side is a mirror image of the other). Cut out the panels using a bandsaw or a fretsaw.

Four strips of wood, measuring 470×8×4 mm, are glued along the inside top and bottom edges of the side panels (see the illustration below). They are positioned 10 mm from the back side of the panel and 90 mm (top edge) and 10 mm (bottom edge) from the front side. The strips stiffen the side panels and provide support for the front panel and the ribs.

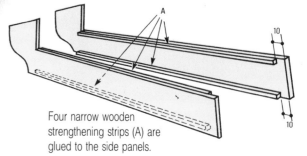

Four narrow wooden strengthening strips (A) are glued to the side panels.

The front panel

The front panel is cut from a piece of wood measuring 120×140×8 mm. Grooves 7 mm wide and 3 mm deep, are cut into the inside surface.

The inside lines of the grooves should be 56 mm apart. They are made with the aid of a tenon saw and a chisel. The tangent case will later be mounted in these grooves.

The tuning pin box and tuning pins

The upper panel of the tuning pin box is cut from a piece of wood measuring 120×140×113 mm. Cut out the panel using a bandsaw or a fretsaw. The positions of the five tuning pin holes are indicated in the illustration. Mark these on the panel using a ruler and compasses. The holes are 12.5 mm in diameter. Drill them out using a 10 mm drill and then open them up to 12.5 mm using a conical gouge.

The upper surface of the panel is rounded slightly with a rasp and sanded smooth.

Buy five cello tuning pins or make your own from your walnut offcuts. They should be 12.5 mm in diameter and 10 cm long. Use a conical sharpener to pare them down to an end diameter of 10 mm. Drill a 1 mm hole close to the narrow end of each pin – though this can

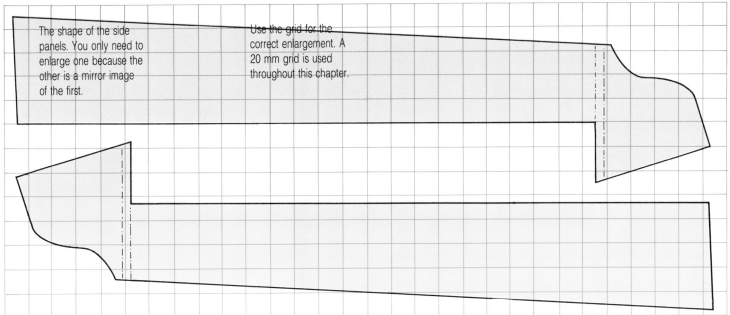

The shape of the side panels. You only need to enlarge one because the other is a mirror image of the first.

Use the grid for the correct enlargement. A 20 mm grid is used throughout this chapter.

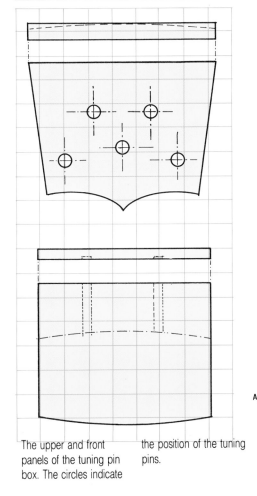

The upper and front panels of the tuning pin box. The circles indicate the position of the tuning pins.

be done later when you are assembling the instrument.

The soundbox

Now that the various parts of the soundbox and tuning pin box have been prepared they are ready to be assembled – as shown in the illustration below. Use a good quality water-based wood glue. First glue strips measuring approximately $10 \times 2 \times 3$ mm inside the side panels (indicated by A in the illustration). These support and strengthen the tuning pin box. Put masking tape around the joints, brush in glue and fit the parts together. Make sure the box is 'square' (not twisted). Secure the pieces in place with the tape and clamps and allow the glue to dry. Clean off any glue remnants and sandpaper all the edges and joints smooth.

The base

A plank measuring $530 \times 150 \times 9$ mm is used to make the base. This plank must be carefully sawn in half to make two planks each 3 mm in thickness. When opened out, the two pieces are more or less identical and the grain runs along the length. Glue the two pieces together, edge to edge, and then glue a thin strip, $530 \times 15 \times 2$ mm, along the joint. The grain of the strip must run across the grain of the two original pieces. This method of making the base is essential to the quality of the eventual sound. It is, however, a difficult operation and it may be better to ask your timber supplier to do the cutting for you.

The top and bottom panels of the soundbox are made from two pieces of wood. The grain of the wood lies along the length. The strip along the middle lies directly over the glued joint.

The illustration shows the assembly of the side panels, tuning pin box and back panel.

Curved wedges are used to hold the bottom panel in place during assembly. Clamps are positioned as indicated by the arrows.

Before this panel is fixed, the edges of the sides must be beveled. The upper drawing shows the under view before the panel is positioned.

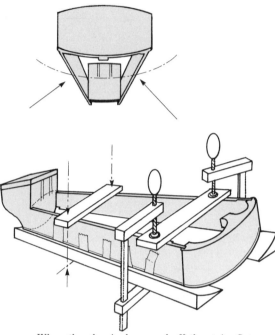

When the glue is dry round off the strip. Set the soundbox on the base panel, draw round it (allow an extra 3 mm all round) and cut it out with a bandsaw. Angle the bottom edges of the side panels to follow the angle of the end panel. The strip on the base is to the inside of the soundbox. Heat the base using a smoothing iron – this will cause it to bow. Now glue it to the soundbox holding it in place with tape. Make concave wedges to help hold the panel in position while the glue is drying (see illustration). Set the wedges and clamps as shown and leave to dry.

The ribs

Cut the ribs A, B, C and D using a jigsaw or a fretsaw according to the illustration on the right.

In ribs A, B and C cut notches 3 mm deep and 3 mm wide in both ends (these sit in pockets cut into the strips in the side panel supports – see illustration right).

Bore holes 3 mm deep and 8 mm in diameter in the center of the undersides of these three ribs. These contain the supporting dowels

which run between the ribs and the base. The curve of the ribs follows the curve of the upper edge of the back panel (see page 109). Holes 20 mm in diameter are bored in ribs A and B as indicated. These hold respectively the axis (A) and the bearing (B).

The axis

The final form of the axis must be exactly as shown in the working drawing. Any good industrial workshop will be able to turn this for you, but you can assemble your own from a flange, bearing and screw assembly purchased at a hardware store.

The size of these parts may vary but this can be allowed for by varying the size of the holes drilled in the ribs. In the example, the length of the axis is geared to the position of the ribs with respect to the back panel. Try to maintain these dimensions.

The bearing, which is mounted in rib B, can be a self-lubricating ball-bearing or a nylon bushing. The screw assembly is mounted in the back panel. The flange is mounted in the wheel. The handle at the end of the axis can be more or less any shape. Some builders cast them in bronze, others cut them from metal or buy them ready-made. The handle of this

instrument was turned from horn but wood or bone can also be used. Ensure that the handle is not too small and that it turns freely.

The wheel

The eventual sound quality of the hurdy gurdy stands or falls with the wheel! The best material to use is delignite. This material consists of thin layers (0.3 mm) of wood glued alternatively crosswise.

You require a piece measuring $180 \times 180 \times 12$ mm. Glue a solid piece of wood, 4 mm in thickness, on each side of this sheet. Using compasses, draw a circle 90 mm in radius on the sheet and cut it out with jigsaw or fretsaw. A hole of the same diameter as that of the flange is bored in the center of the wheel with an auger. Of course, the wheel can be cut roughly to shape and then finished on a lathe. This operation calls for some expertise (not to mention a lathe!). If you possess neither it may be better to have the wheel made by a professional wood turner. If you do this, take with you the axis, the soundbox and the drawing showing the shapes and sizes. Lastly the sides of the wheel are slightly rounded (see illustration page 118). The flange is sunk unto the wheel and screwed in place.

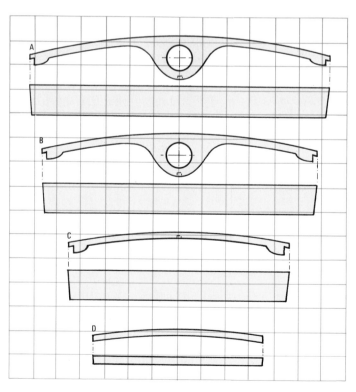

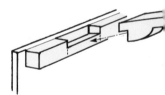

The illustration shows the shapes of the ribs (views from the front and above). D is the rib which is glued to the tuning pin box.
The way in which the ribs are joined to the side panels is shown above.

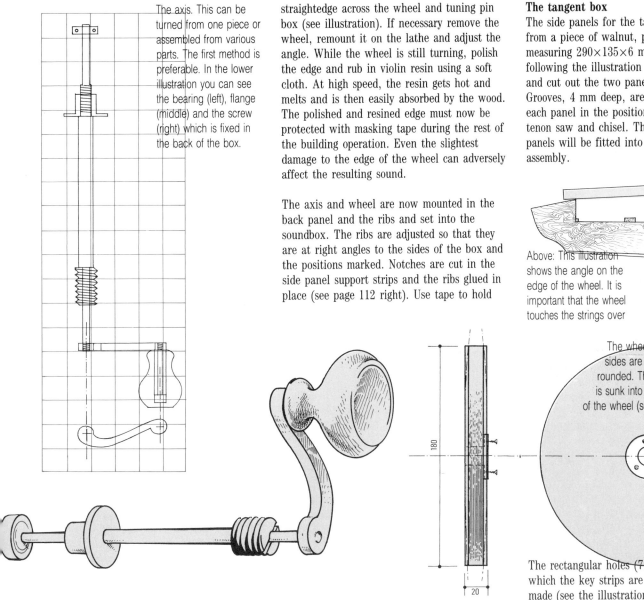

The axis. This can be turned from one piece or assembled from various parts. The first method is preferable. In the lower illustration you can see the bearing (left), flange (middle) and the screw (right) which is fixed in the back of the box.

straightedge across the wheel and tuning pin box (see illustration). If necessary remove the wheel, remount it on the lathe and adjust the angle. While the wheel is still turning, polish the edge and rub in violin resin using a soft cloth. At high speed, the resin gets hot and melts and is then easily absorbed by the wood. The polished and resined edge must now be protected with masking tape during the rest of the building operation. Even the slightest damage to the edge of the wheel can adversely affect the resulting sound.

The axis and wheel are now mounted in the back panel and the ribs and set into the soundbox. The ribs are adjusted so that they are at right angles to the sides of the box and the positions marked. Notches are cut in the side panel support strips and the ribs glued in place (see page 112 right). Use tape to hold

The tangent box

The side panels for the tangent box are made from a piece of walnut, pear or plum measuring 290×135×6 mm. Make a template following the illustration on page 114, draw and cut out the two panels.

Grooves, 4 mm deep, are cut on the inside of each panel in the positions indicated using a tenon saw and chisel. The front and back panels will be fitted into these grooves during assembly.

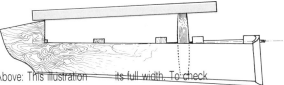

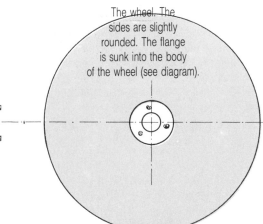

Above: This illustration shows the angle on the edge of the wheel. It is important that the wheel touches the strings over its full width. To check this lay a ruler across the wheel and the tuning pin box.

The wheel. The sides are slightly rounded. The flange is sunk into the body of the wheel (see diagram).

The rectangular holes (7×5 mm) through which the key strips are mounted must now be made (see the illustration and table at the bottom of page 114). The positions are determined using a steel ruler and try square. The holes run parallel to the top edge of the panels. They are cut as follows: first mark the center points by drawing in the diagonals – the center is at the point where the diagonals cross. Make starter holes with an awl. Clamp the two side panels, one on top of the other, to a wooden base and mount the whole in a drill stand. Drill out the holes, using a 5 mm drill. Remove the panels from the stand and square off the holes to the required size using a flat 5 mm key file or a paring chisel. Now bore three 1 mm holes, roughly 70 mm apart,

Now mount the axis and wheel in the ribs and transfer the whole assembly to the soundboux.

The position of the wheel

The angle of the wheel and its distance from the tuning pin box are of the utmost importance. The distance is important because this provides the scale of the instrument – the length of the vibrating string – and it must be exactly 343 mm. The angle at which the edge of the wheel is set is important because the strings must touch the entire width of the wheel.

The angle can be determined by setting a

these joints in place as the glue dries. Rib D is glued to the front of the tuning pin box. Ribs A, B and C are supported by lengths of dowel, 8 mm in diameter, positioned between the holes in the undersides of the ribs and the base panel (see page 115).

Hurdy gurdy and bagpipes players from Auvergne, France, around 1900.

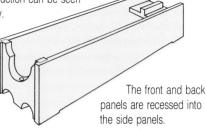

The parts of the tangent box. The grid allows you to enlarge these to the required size.

The tangent box. The construction can be seen clearly.

The front panel of the tangent box is set back 3 mm to allow the sides to fit into the grooves in the tuning pin box.

The front and back panels are recessed into the side panels.

about 5 mm below the top edge of one of the side panels. These will be needed later when the lid of the tangent box is attached.

The front panel of the tangent box is made from a piece of wood measuring 64×30×7 mm and the back panel from a piece measuring 70×64×12 mm. Again make a template to draw these shapes before you cut them out. A 3 mm hole is drilled through the center of the back panel (see illustration). The top of the hole is then countersunk using a 5 mm drill. This is for the screw which attaches the tangent box to the soundbox.

The edge of the front panel of the tangent box butts up against the front panel of the tuning pin box.

The pieces of the tangent box can now be assembled. Use a try square to ensure the panels are at right angles, then glue and clamp them together. Let the glue dry and then sandpaper the whole box smooth.

Positioning the strips on which the tangents are fixed. These holes are cut into the sides of the tangent box.

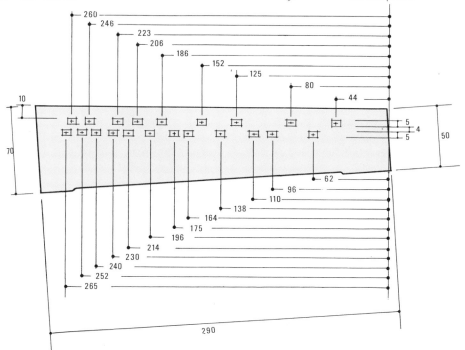

The tangent box lid measures $290\times70\times8$ mm. Round off the upper surface. Drill three 1 mm holes in the lid to coincide with those drilled in the side panel.

When the instrument is finally assembled, the lid can be attached by means of cord or wire 'hinges'. Note: Do not use metal hinges as they tend to distort the sound.

The keyboard

Strips of wood of cross-section 5×7 mm are used for the key strips. Choose a fine-grained hardwood, such as maple, box wood or ebony. There are twenty-one key strips altogether and you need a length of about 210 cm. Cut nine 88 mm strips and twelve 95 mm strips.

The keys themselves are made from keyboard strips, one measuring $270\times15\times8$ mm, the other $270\times7\times20$ mm.

Cut a groove 5 mm wide and 4 mm deep in the first strip, using a circular saw.

Similarly, cut a groove 5 mm wide and 13 mm deep in the second (see illustration).

The tangents. These are later mounted in the key strips. Cut them from a molding or a sheet of PVC.

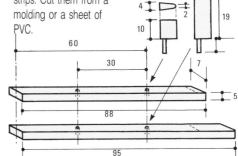

Round off the strips as indicated in the illustration using a rasp and sandpaper. Lay the tangent box on its side on a flat surface and insert the key strips in the holes. Glue one keyboard strip to the key strips and allow the glue to dry. Then glue on the second keyboard strip. Study the illustration at the bottom of page 116 and the photograph of the model on pages 108-109 very carefully and then cut out the individual keys – first from

This exploded drawing shows all the parts of the hurdy gurdy and how they fit together.

one keyboard strip and then the other – using a fretsaw. Finish the keys off with very fine sandpaper.

Two holes, 3 mm in diameter, are drilled in each key strip as indicated in the illustration on page 115. Determine the positions of the holes using a steel ruler. The tangents are mounted in these.

The tangents can be made from a hardwood such as maple, ebony or box wood or from a sheet of pvc plastic 3.5 mm thick. If you are using hardwood, the tangents are drawn and then cut out and shaped as indicated in the illustration. You may be able to purchase pvc in the required profile. There are 42 tangents alltogether – 18 of 10 mm with a stem of 5 mm, and 24 of 19 mm also with a stem of 5 mm. All the tangents are 10 mm in width and 4 mm tapering to 2 mm in thickness. The tangents are mounted in the holes in the key strips. They must fit tightly but at the same time you must be able to turn them from side to side. The instrument can be finely tuned by altering the angle of the tangents. Finally, the tangent box is treated with a coat of teak or white furniture oil.

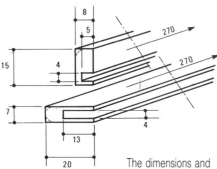

The keys are made from two grooved strips of good quality hardwood. The dimensions and position of the holes in the strips in which the tangents which stop the strings are mounted.

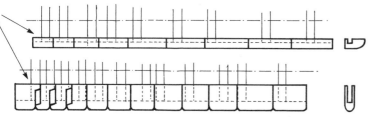

All dimensions are in millimetres

The view of the keys from above shows the shape of each key separately.

The string holder

The string holder is made from a piece of wood measuring approx. 25×50×120 mm. Draw the shape and cut it out. Drill a hole, 7 mm in diameter, in the position indicated. This is for the trumpet string tuning key. Round it out to a diameter of 9 mm using a conical gouge. The tuning pin can either be a ready-made violin pin or one you have made yourself.
Now drill 1 mm holes, 30 mm apart and 20 mm deep, in the end of the string holder. Drill 2 mm holes in the underside to the base of these two holes (the finished holes are L-shaped – see illustration).
Drill a 2 mm hole between these two holes for the wire which attaches the string holder to the bridge. Drill 6 mm holes to hold the pegs which attach the string holder to the body. Round off the top of the string holder using a plane and rasp and sandpaper it smooth.

The bridges

There are three bridges on the hurdy gurdy – one for the melody strings, one for the bourdon strings and one for the trumpet string. The bridge for the melody strings is made from a piece of maple measuring 70×66×10 mm. Cut this out with a fretsaw according to the model in the illustration. Sandpaper it smooth and taper it with a plane and rasp. The top edge should be 2 mm and the bottom edge 8-9 mm in thickness. The grooves in the top edge are 30 mm apart.

The bridge for the bourdon strings is made from a piece of wood measuring 40×30×8 mm. Cut the piece out according to the illustration using a fretsaw and then shape it with a small rasp. Cut grooves as indicated. This bridge is used to lift the bourdon strings from the wheel which not only allows variations in sound but also means that it is much easier to tune the melody strings.

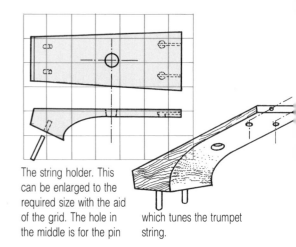

The string holder. This can be enlarged to the required size with the aid of the grid. The hole in the middle is for the pin which tunes the trumpet string.

The bridge for the trumpet string has the same basic shape as that for the bourdons but has no grooves. The head is cut away slightly and a groove, 2 mm wide, is cut into the head using a small tenon saw and a fine rasp (see the dotted lines in F in the illustration on page 117). The 'dog' is cut from a piece of scrap wood. Cut a groove for the string and file the tongue until it fits the groove in the head. Sandpaper both pieces smooth. When the wheel is turned rapidly, the dog moves in and out of the head, striking the soundbox and producing a staccato sound.

The travel pin for the trumpet string

The travel pin for the trumpet string is positioned directly above rib B. You can use a ready-made drawer knob but it is a simple enough matter to turn your own on a lathe. When the trumpet string is led around this pin, it does not touch the wheel. This makes it possible to play different combinations of strings and also helps you to tune the strings individually.

The cap

A protective cap, supported between two wooden strips, is positioned over the wheel in order to prevent any possible damage. The support strips are cut from pieces of wood measuring 14×5×80 mm. These can actually be made from ready-made molding and colored with varnish – but this is not really an ideal solution to the problem.
The best thing is to try and find remnants of maple or walnut to make these pieces.
Cut the protective cap from plywood or a thin

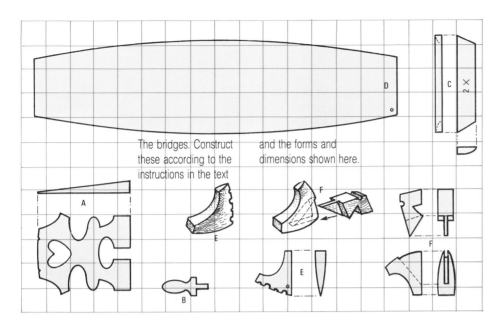

The bridges. Construct these according to the instructions in the text and the forms and dimensions shown here.

A. The bridge. This is cut from a piece of maple wood according to the illustration. Use the grid to enlarge the bridge to the required size. Notice that one side is tapered (see also illustration p. 118).

B. A drawer knob can be used as the travel pin for the trumpet string, but we suggest you turn your own.

C. The supports for the protective cap are made from scrap wood.

D. The protective cap for the wheel is made from thin plywood. This is set in boiling water and then bent to the required shape.

E. The bridge for the bourdon strings. This is filed from a piece of wood 3×4 cm and 8 mm in thickness.

F. The bridge for the trumpet string is more complex as it consists of two parts. The first is similar to the bourdon string bridge but has a small piece removed and a groove cut into it to hold the second part.

sheet of walnut measuring 300×80×2 mm. In one corner drill a hole with a diameter of approximately 2 mm. This is necessary for the cord which will later attach the cap to the soundbox.

Lay the cap in boiling water for five minutes or so, remove it carefully and bend it over a round mold which is a little larger than the wheel. Attach the cap securely to the mold – with a clamp or strong cord, for example, and allow it to dry out thoroughly. If you have a metal former in your workshop, you can make the correct shape in a few minutes.

The upper panel

The basic form of the upper panel is made in the same way as that for the base (see page 111) and thus consists of two parts. A beautiful panel is obtained by using quarter-sawn pine, maple or walnut wood. Offer the wheel assembly up to the panel and mark very carefully where the opening must be positioned. Cut it out using a fretsaw. The finished opening should be 2 or 3 mm wider and broader than the wheel – in other words there should be a clearance of 1 mm on all sides of the wheel. The sound holes (see the model in the photograph on pages 108-109) are also cut at this stage. When all the parts have been positioned in the soundbox the upper panel can be glued in place. Most instrument builders attach a name plate to the inside of the base – you may care to do the same!

Plane or rasp the top edges of the side panels until they are at a slight angle. Fix the panel in position with strong tape. Use wedges and clamps (see page 112) to hold it in place while the glue dries.

Fitting the other parts

All the edges, joints and surfaces are now sanded smooth and all traces of glue removed. Furniture or instrument oil is rubbed into all the surfaces. If you wish, you can varnish the instrument instead. The oil must be well absorbed into the wood which is why it is applied before the smaller parts are mounted. The oil or varnish is then scraped or sanded away from the surface where the parts are to be fitted. Glue the string holder in position. This is strengthened by plugs sunk into the back panel.

The top panel of the soundbox is made in the same way as the bottom panel. The opening for the wheel is 2-3 mm larger than the wheel itself.

The tangent box, the travel pin, the cap supports and the bourdon and trumpet string bridges are fixed in position. The tangent box and travel pin are glued and screwed in position. The cap supports and bridges are only glued. Traces of glue or oil must be removed from the surface before the parts are glued in place.

The strings

The hurdy gurdy has five strings: two melody strings, a trumpet string, a thick bourdon string and a thin bourdon string. Special hurdy gurdy strings can be bought in specialist stores but viola, harp or gamba strings can also be used. If there is no alternative, even nylon strings can be used. (See string table on page 119.)

Small holes, through which the strings are led, are bored in the tuning pin box. There is insufficient space for the body of a drill and so you must make your own flexible bit from a length of steel wire of diameter 2 mm. Cut the head of the wire off as shown in the diagram below. The holes for the trumpet string and the thick bourdon string lie 11 mm above the upper panel of the soundbox. The hole for the thin bourdon string lies 10 mm above that for the thick string.

The three string holders for the trumpet and bourdon strings consist of U-shaped staples set into the back panel. Make these from 2 mm wire and attach them as indicated in the diagram. Drawer knobs and similar ready-made parts usually make excellent string holders, but in this case they can hinder the turning of the handle and are therefore unsuitable.

The melody strings run from the separate string holder via the tangent box to the tuning pin box. Attach these strings to the string holder as indicated.

The melody strings pass through two holes in the tuning pin box. They are brought to the correct height by means of two hardwood or bone bridges, 20 mm wide and 5 mm in thickness, which are fitted to the cross piece at the end of the tangent box (see illustration). The height of the bridges depends on the positions of the holes – remember that the 'scale' of this instrument – the distance between the wheel and the tuning box – is 343 mm.

Now mount the bridge for the melody strings in the position indicated – just behind the wheel. The bridge is not glued but is held in position by the tension of the strings. The tapered side of the bridge faces the back of the instrument – the handle. The bridge is attached to the string holder by an S-shaped wire (see illustration). Mount both melody strings together so that the string holder cannot be pulled out of position. The trumpet string is attached to the tuning pin by a separate length of string so that it can be tuned.

And finally...

Finally absorbant cotton or silk thread is wrapped tightly round the strings where they pass over the wheel.

Ready-made drawer knobs (or knobs you have turned on a lathe) are now attached to the front and back of the instrument for the shoulder strap. Make this strap from a length of leather 50 to 80 mm in width. The length of the strap varies from person to person. When the instrument is finally assembled, the protective tape is removed from the wheel. It is now ready to be tuned.

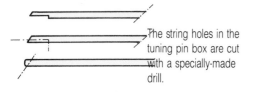

The string holes in the tuning pin box are cut with a specially-made drill.

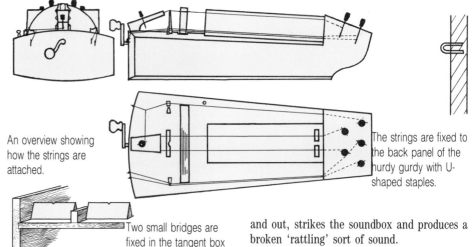

An overview showing how the strings are attached.

The strings are fixed to the back panel of the hurdy gurdy with U-shaped staples.

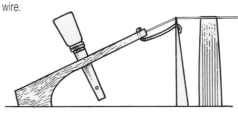

Two small bridges are fixed in the tangent box behind the tuning pin box. The height of the bridges determines the positions of the string holes in the tuning pin box.

The large bridge is positioned with its tapered side towards the wheel and fixed to the string holder with a metal wire.

Tuning the hurdy gurdy

Adjusting and tuning the hurdy gurdy is an almost impossible task – if you are doing it for the very first time! We therefore advise you to find someone with experience to show you 'the tricks of the trade'. The following instructions give you only an indication of the procedure.

The tuning of the hurdy gurdy is carried out in two stages – firstly by tensioning the strings, and secondly by adjusting the tangents. The melody strings are tuned first, then the trumpet string and lastly the thin and thick bourdon strings.

The melody strings should have an equally loud, clear sound. When this is so, the tangents can be adjusted.

The trumpet string is tuned to the same pitch as the melody strings. When the instrument is played at normal speed, this string produces a pure sound but when the handle is turned more rapidly, the dog in the bridge moves in and out, strikes the soundbox and produces a broken 'rattling' sort of sound.

The thin bourdon string is tuned one octave lower than the melody and trumpet strings. The thick bourdon is tuned a further fifth below that. Both bourdons must be audible. The greater the tension in the strings, the louder their volume. If the bourdons tend to drown out the melody strings, then the melody string bridge can be made a little thinner. The last fine tuning is carried out by adjusting the angle of the tangents.

There are specialist books on the market which explain this procedure in detail.

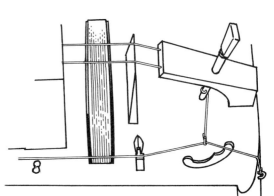

The trumpet string is tensioned via a string by the tuning pin in the string holder.

Playing the hurdy gurdy

There is no hard and fast method of fingering this instrument. The keyboard is played with the little, ring, middle and index fingers of the left hand which moves freely over the lid of the tangent box. As a basic rule the same finger is never – or as seldom as possible – used to play two consecutive notes, with the exception of 'riffs'. The wheel is turned with the right hand. Every hurdy gurdy has its own character and the expression 'learning by doing' applies when learning to play this instrument.

Seek the advice of someone who has some experience of playing the instrument. It is also a good idea to purchase a book on the subject. Practise and perseverence are the two basic formulae in learning to play this fascinating instrument.

Stringing

	DO tuning gut strings		SO tuning gut strings	
melody strings	SO of the G clef	RE (violin) MI (harp) no. 15	RE of the G clef	RE (viola) RE (harp) no. 16
trumpet string	SO of the G clef	RE (violin) MI (harp) no. 15	RE of the G clef	RE (viola) RE (harp) no. 16
thin bourdon	SO, octave under the melody	LA (cello)	RE, octave below the melody	SO wound from cello
thick bourdon	DO, fifth below thin bourdon	SO wound from cello	SOL, fifth below thin bourdon	DO wound from cello

With the DO tuning, the instrument is played in the key of C and C minor. To play in G and G minor the thick bourdon only must be lifted from the wheel.

With the SO tuning the instrument is played in the key of G and G minor. To play in the key of D and D minor the thick bourdon only must be lifted from the wheel.

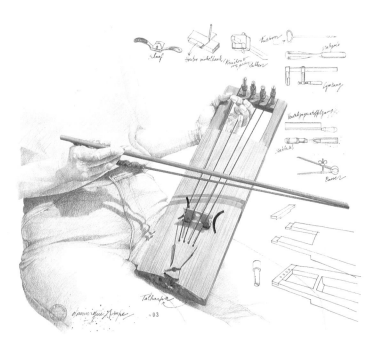

Bibliography

Muziek op hakkebord en klompviool, *Herman Dewit,* Vereniging Buma/Stichting Stemra.

Encyclopedia of musical instruments, *Diagram Visual Information Ltd. Paddington Press Ltd./Atrium.*

Draaailierboek, *Herman Dewit and Toon Moonen,* Vereniging voor Huismuziek.

Muziekinstrumenten zelf maken, *Kurt Schweizer and Susanne Bosshard,* Elmar Creatief.

How to play nearly everything, *Dallas Cline,* Oak Publications.

Folk Instruments, *Dennis Waring,* Hyperion Press Limited.

De Hommel, *Hubert Boone,* Instrument museum and Musicological Research Assocation, Distributor Frits Knuf.

De geschiedenis van de muziekinstrumenten, *Curt Sachs,* Aula.

The Bowed-Harp, *Otto Andersson,* AMS Press.

Van vedelaars, trommers en pijpers, *Mr. J.E. Spruit,* A. Oosthoek's Uitgeversmij NV.

Volksmuziekatelier Jaarboek 1, *Provinciaal trefcentrum Baljuwhuis,* Galmaarden.

De viool, *Eduard Melkus,* Uitgeverij Helmond/Standaard Uitgeverij.

Instruments of popular music, *Lilla M. Fox,* Lutterworth Press.

Het Midwinterhoornblazen, *Everhard Jans,* Twents-Gelderse Uitgeverij Witkam bv.

De mondtrom, *Hubert Boone,* Uitgeverij La Renaissance du Livre.

La Vielle à Roue, *Luce Moïses,* Editions la Renaissance du Livre.

De doedelzak in de wereld, *Provinciaal trefcentrum Baljuwhuis,* Galmaarden.

European and American Musical Instruments, *Anthony Baines,* B.T. Batsford Ltd.

Ethnic Musical Instruments, *Jean Jenkins,* Hugh Evelyn for the International Council of Museums.

Saiteninstrumente selbst gebaut, *Martin Kesselring,* Zytglogge Verlag Bern.

Volksmuziek en volksinstrumenten in Europa, *R.J.M. van Acht,* Haags Gemeentemuseum.

Op harpen en snaren, Uitgeverij de Nederlanden.

Acknowledgements

This book was made in close cooperation with the Flemish folk musician Herman Dewit and the Dutch street musician Hans Goddefroy. Together with his wife Rosita Tahon, his brother-in-law Oswald Tahon and Wilfried Moonen, Herman Dewit is a member of the folk groep 't Kliekske'. This group has produced several long-playing records. Herman Dewit has a high reputation among folk musicians as a builder of quality instruments. He is dedicated, by means of practical courses and working seminars, to the preservation of this dying craft.

As a street musician Hans Goddefroy, with his wife Mechel, plays a wide variety of folk instruments. The couple have also given folk concerts throughout the world.

Most of the models featured in this book have been made, or lent, by Herman Dewit and Hans Goddefroy. Instruments borrowed from others are credited in caption.

Illustration Acknowledgements

Photo research: Beeldbank & Uitgeefprojekten bv, Amsterdam.

Johannes Odé, Rotterdam	p. 6, 49, 50/51
Annie Tillema, Warfhuizen	p. 28
Beeldbank & Uitgeefprojekten bv, Amsterdam	p. 31
H.H. Warncke, Neuss	p. 34
Henk van der Leeden, Marken	p. 44
Centraal Museum, Utrecht	p. 67
Ludo Kuipers, Harlingen	p. 70
Jan Zwart, Amsterdam	p. 75
Thijs Koobs, Amsterdam	p. 79
H. Magr, Emmerich	p. 93

Herman Dewit, Kester, Belgium, for engravings and photos of hurdy gurdy players.
Photography models: Jack Botermans, Drimmelen, the Netherlands.
Working drawings: Piet Hohmann, Oosterhout, the Netherlands.

D

JL

Jl